THE POPE
AND THE
HERETIC

Also by Michael White

Tolkien: A Biography

Isaac Newton: The Last Sorcerer

Leonardo: The First Scientist

Stephen Hawking: A Life in Science *(with John Gribbin)*

Einstein: A Life in Science *(with John Gribbin)*

Darwin: A Life in Science *(with John Gribbin)*

The Science of the X-Files

Super Science

Life Out There

Newton

Galileo

John Lennon

Mozart

Breakthrough *(with Kevin Davies)*

Weird Science

Alien Life Forms

Mind and Matter

Asimov: The Unauthorised Biography

Thompson Twin: An '80s Memoir

Acid Tongues and Tranquil Dreamers

THE POPE

AND THE

HERETIC

The True Story of Giordano Bruno, the Man

Who Dared to Defy the Roman Inquisition

MICHAEL WHITE

WILLIAM MORROW

An In shers

HarperCollins books may be purchased for educational,
business, or sales promotional use. For information
please write: Special Markets Department, HarperCollins
Publishers Inc., 10 East 53rd Street, New York, NY 10022.

FIRST EDITION

Designed by Victoria Hartman

Printed on acid-free paper

Library of Congress Cataloging-in-Publication Data
White, Michael, 1959–
The pope and the heretic : the true story of Giordano Bruno, the man who dared
to defy the Roman Inquisition / Michael White.—1st ed.
p.   cm.
Includes bibliographical references and index.
ISBN 0-06-018626-7
1. Bruno, Giordano, 1548–1600.   2. Philosophers—Italy—Biography.
3. Heretics, Christian—Italy—Biography.   I. Title.
B783.Z7 W53 2002
195—dc21
[B]   2001044050

02   03   04   05   06   WBC/RRD   10   9   8   7   6   5   4   3   2   1

For our son, Noah Isaac,

born May 10, 2000

My Thoughts are stitched to the stars.

—John Lily

CONTENTS

Contents

ACKNOWLEDGMENTS

For the author, there are many pleasures that come from writing: the thrill of creativity, the buzz of receiving the first copy of a new book, the paycheck. But another is the moment after the manuscript is written when I can thank everyone who had a hand in its creation.

First, I would like to say thank you to my agents, Russ Galen and Peter Robinson, whose faith in this project kept me going when the world seemed against my writing it. Also, I would like to show my appreciation to my editors on each side of the Atlantic, Andrew Gordon and Alan Samson in London and Jennifer Brehl in New York. I also owe thanks to the staff of the Doges' Palace in Venice and the Castel Sant'Angelo in the Vatican, the helpful librarians at the British Library, London, and those at Museo Correr, Venice.

Finally, as always, I would like to thank my wife, Lisa, who endured my going to Italy without her, and our children, India, George, and Noah, who had to put up with many bathtimes without Daddy.

Michael White, March 2002

INTRODUCTION

Time gives all and takes all away; everything changes, but
nothing perishes.

—Giordano Bruno

THE GHOST OF Giordano Bruno has been hanging over me
for years. He is one of those historical figures who keep
turning up, Zelig-like, in what, at least on the surface, appear to be
other people's stories. I first encountered Bruno while writing *The
Last Sorcerer*, a biography of Isaac Newton. He appeared as a writer
and mystic, one of the cadre of individuals who had helped to
popularize the Hermetic tradition, the lore of the occult. Newton
was fascinated with this secret knowledge and had read Bruno's
work before embarking upon his own arcane studies and alchemical experiments.

Then later, while I was researching an entirely different book
called *Life Out There*, concerned with the search for life on other
planets, Giordano Bruno popped up again. It turned out he had a
great deal to say about the possibility of intelligent extraterrestrials,
and this, coming from a figure of the sixteenth century, fascinated

me. Some time later, I moved on to a biography of Leonardo da Vinci, *Leonardo: The First Scientist*, and there was Bruno again, a torchbearer for the sort of holistic dreams Leonardo cherished. Bruno, it turned out, was a blend of the mystic, the philosopher, and the scientist and wrote about a form of unification, a coagulation of all disciplines to create an overarching vision, just as Leonardo had before him and Newton would after him.

But of course, Bruno was not just another philosopher interested in an assortment of ideas. To me, it now seemed clear that this man was someone working at the very heart of intellectual life during the Renaissance and that he had stood at a crossroads in the evolution of human thought. Bruno was alive with a fervor to know and to explore. He perceived no boundaries and accepted no limitations. He was superintelligent and vastly erudite, but he was not a specialist, not a genius of a single discipline. Bruno's was an intelligence of the kind that sought out challenging, dangerous ideas and found links among them, but most important, he had the guts and determination to proselytize his conclusions in an age rancid with persecution and corrupted piety.

As a young man Bruno acquired the nickname "the Nolan," which derived from his birthplace of Nola near Naples in southern Italy. He began life as a simple priest but left his order and was excommunicated on suspicion of heresy. The remainder of his life was spent wandering across Europe, teaching and writing. He never stayed anywhere for more than two years, yet he produced dozens of books and papers and was patronized by some of the most powerful figures of his day, including Henry III of France and Elizabeth I of England. For a short time he was employed as a spy at the English court, and he knew personally many of the most famous (and often notorious) alchemists, cabalists, and mystics of the age. He was a fiery, difficult, argumentative man; brave, certainly, but abrasive.

After almost a quarter of a century as an itinerant, Bruno returned to Italy. Within months he was arrested by the Inquisition and tried as a heretic. Then, after enduring almost eight years of imprisonment, first in Venice and then in Rome, and repeated torture at the hands of the cardinals, he was burned at the stake in Rome.

Bruno's murder was condemned by liberal thinkers across Europe, and it added yet another mark of ignominy to the already black names of the Inquisition and the Papal Office. Not surprisingly, the Vatican did its very best to conceal details of Bruno's trial and the process of his persecution. For this reason, until relatively recent times, little was known about the final eight years of Bruno's life and the mechanism of his trials.

Bruno was tried first in Venice and then in Rome. The records of the Venetian trial and a fragment of the Roman proceedings were discovered between 1844 and 1848 in the Vatican Archives, almost 250 years after his execution. These were published for the first time in 1849 as an appendix to a book about the Copernican heliocentric system by a scholar named Domenico Berti. Berti later wrote the first biography of Bruno, *Vita di Giordano Bruno da Nola* (1868).

These accounts gave a detailed picture of the Venetian trial during May and June 1592 but provided only snapshots of the eight years Bruno spent in the prisons of the Inquisition in the

Vatican and the procedure against him during those years. It is now believed that most of the material pertaining to those years was lost when Napoleon's troops ransacked the Vatican in 1798 and returned to France with documents snatched indiscriminately from the Papal Libraries.

But not everything was lost. In 1925, a cardinal named Angelo Mercati became prefect of the Secret Vatican Archives and learned of some documents relating to the Roman trial of Bruno that had been unearthed nearly forty years earlier, in 1887. To Mercati's astonishment, he discovered that the then pope, Leo X, had at the time ordered that the documents be sent to him immediately and their contents revealed to no one.

Intrigued, Mercati continued to delve, and by 1940 he had found the lost documents in the personal archives of Pope Pius XI, who had died the year before. Because these documents describe the final trials and the pronouncement of sentence on Bruno, they offered great insight for Bruno scholars, but sadly they detailed only Bruno's appearances before the Inquisition in Rome between 1597 and his execution in February 1600 and said little about the first six years of his internment. In 1940, Cardinal Mercati published the material under the title *Il sommario del processo di Giordano Bruno,* and this remains the most detailed report of the proceedings against Bruno and the exchange of arguments between the Nolan and the cardinals that led to a verdict.

Since then, other historians have gradually revealed aspects of Giordano's life and work. The great writer on the Hermetic tradition the late Dame Frances Yates added much to the canon of knowledge about Bruno's philosophy with her book *The Art of*

Memory, and more recently, Hilary Gatti has analyzed Bruno's contribution to the natural philosophy of his time in her *Giordano Bruno and Renaissance Science.* Yet much about Bruno remains a mystery. His writing style is rooted very much in the time in which he lived, and to modern readers it often seems clumsy and his meaning obscure. As for his life, it comes to us as a patchwork in which some incidents are recorded well, while long stretches are veiled, lost from history altogether.

This, then, is a tale of persecution, the story of a fight, a battle between unequal forces in which one man made a stand against ignorance, dogma, and corruption. Rallied against him was the temporal might of an entire religion, whose representatives, Pope Clement VIII and his cardinals, deemed it necessary to burn Giordano. Yet, as we shall see, theirs was a Pyrrhic victory, ultimately the actions of desperate men. Their day was drawing to a close, while the memory and significance of the man whose body they obliterated would become increasingly important with each passing year.

THE POPE
AND THE
HERETIC

· I ·

PRELUDE TO A BURNING

For large wood: 55 sols 6 deniers
For vine-branches: 21 sols 3 deniers
For straw: 2 sols 6 deniers
For four stakes: 10 sols 9 deniers
For ropes to tie the convicts: 45 sols 7 deniers
For the executioners, each 20 sols: 80 sols.
——Inquisition accounts for an execution

THE GRAND INQUISITOR, the Lord Cardinal Santoro di Santa Severina, was not happy. It was freezing cold in the Congregation Chamber of the Vatican, and he remembered fondly the attentions of his lover earlier that morning. His hair disheveled, his limbs aching, he had been called from those attentions and reminded (with suitable reverence) that he must wash and dress and follow his servants to the Hall of the Congregation and the trial of the reviled heretic Giordano Bruno.

And now Father Bruno, a small man with black hair and dark brown eyes, stood before him, wafer-thin, scarred and drained, his face and body bearing the marks of the Inquisition.[1] The date was

---

1. Although Bruno had been excommunicated, he was still referred to in official documents as Fr. Bruno.

February 8, 1600, and Giordano Bruno had less than eleven days to live.

The hall was vast and ornate. The eight cardinals and the seven coadjutors and notaries sat on comfortable high-backed chairs forming an arc around the accused, their official robes of satin falling gently over their velvet seats. The Lord Cardinal Severina was seated in a giant throne at the apex of the arc, his hands placed on the ornate wooden arms, his long bony fingers twitching with impatience, his cardinal ring bobbing and catching the light streaming in from long windows that dominated an entire wall of the chamber behind him.

Of the cardinals at this meeting, only two were truly important. First there was Cardinal Severina himself. Pope Clement VIII's right-hand man had never recovered from his failure to secure the papacy for himself immediately before Bruno's first imprisonment in Venice eight years earlier. Arrogant and egotistical, Severina had been so confident of his destiny he had already selected his official name; ironically he had planned to use Clement. And now he loathed the real Clement more than he could have imagined. He knew the pope was inclined to be lenient with Bruno; it seemed the fool had some inexplicable soft spot for him, and so Severina would do everything he could to oppose Clement and to hurt Bruno.

The other cardinal to be feared was Robert Bellarmine, a man who would have liked to see not just heretics but all Protestants and dissenters burned, all traces of anti-Catholic feeling expunged. Bellarmine had been a professor of theology at the Collegium Romanum and had been given the honor of becoming personal theologian to the pope, the Holy See's adviser on all matters of doctrine, keeper of the Word. For all his academic brilliance, Robert Bellarmine's worldview was strictly antiscience. Fifteen years after Bruno was in his grave, the reverend cardinal would instigate the arrest and trial of Galileo. As reward, the Church would canonize Bellarmine in 1930.

Bruno stood in silence before the fifteen men. Severina read the charges, a total of eight counts of heresy. These included his belief that the transubstantiation of bread into flesh and wine into blood was a falsehood, that the virgin birth was impossible, and, perhaps most terrible of all, that we live in an infinite universe and that innumerable worlds exist upon which creatures like ourselves might thrive and worship their own gods.

Against these charges, Bruno refused to comment. He would, he said, address himself only to His Holiness personally. The Congregation had a written statement from Bruno to Clement which Bellarmine had opened but had no intention of showing the pope, disclosing as it did details of Bruno's heretical ideas.

With an outward display of patience and piety, Cardinal Severina again asked Bruno if he was prepared to recant his heresies, but Bruno simply stared at the wall behind the row of cardinals and remained silent. And so, with a heavy, theatrical sigh, Severina sat back, placed his palms on the arms of his throne, and glanced quickly to his left, toward Bellarmine.

For a moment the room was absolutely silent, then slowly Severina leaned forward again and read a prepared statement from His Holiness Pope Clement VIII:

"I decree and commend that the cause should be carried to

extreme measures, *servatus servandis* [with all due formalities], sentence should be pronounced and the said Brother Giordanus be committed to the secular court."

And with that pronouncement, Bruno was led from the room to face further torture.

Later that same day, Giordano Bruno stood once more facing a semicircle of judges. This time he had been called before a secular committee headed by the governor of Rome in the Hall of the Inquisition at the Monastery of Minerva.

This hearing was called because the Holy See never sentenced heretics to the stake directly; with characteristic hypocrisy it always passed that duty on to a civil authority. The official statement from the Holy Office to the governor of Rome was invariable:

"Take him [the heretic] under your jurisdiction, subject to your decision, so as to be punished with the due chastisement; beseeching you, however, as we do earnestly beseech you, so to mitigate the severity of your sentence with respect to his body that there may be no danger of death or of the shedding of blood. So we Cardinals, Inquisitor and General, whose names are written beneath decree."[2]

---

2. Vatican Archives, Doc. Rom. xxvi. Some of these archives and the documents from the Venetian Inquisition were first published in Vincenzo Spampanato, *Vita di Giordano Bruno* (Messina, 1921), pp. 599–786. These were later used by Giovanni Gentile in *Documenti della vita di Giordano Bruno* (Florence, 1933). These documents were supplemented by Mercati's findings published in 1942 as *Il sommario del processo di Giordano Bruno* (Vatican City, 1942).

This statement was effectively an order to the secular court. They were to take Bruno and burn him alive. Through the centuries, successive governors and judges never once demurred from this disguised papal demand, never once commuted the sentence, because if they had ever decided to ignore the instruction of the Holy Office, they would have been instantly excommunicated and perhaps have found themselves facing death without "the shedding of blood."

And so, with Bruno on his knees before his judges, the governor of Rome passed sentence. The bishop of Sidonia, who had been paid a fee of twenty-seven scudi for the privilege, stepped forward, stripped the robe from Bruno's back, ripped his priest's insignia from him, and condemned his soul to suffer the perpetual flames of Hell, symbolically degrading his spirit just as the flames would degrade his physical body. The cardinals and the secular judges wanted to erase the very essence of this heretic, just as of all heretics.[3] They wanted to pretend this man had never lived. With great ceremony, they would burn his work and burn his body, dissolve his spirit and powder his physical being.

With the bishop's words of doom still ringing in the great chamber, sentence of death at the stake was passed, and the governor asked Bruno if he had anything to say.

For long moments there was again no sound in the room. The

---

3. Doc. Rom. xxxiii. In almost all ways this was a ritual with the sole purpose of demeaning and humiliating Bruno ceremonially because he had been excommunicated and therefore cast out of the Church many years earlier. It must be assumed that Bruno had been dressed in priest's robes specifically for this ritualistic disrobing.

judges and the clergy stared at the broken man, looking now like a mere heap of rags on the marble floor. Then Bruno lifted his head, surveyed the room almost insouciantly, and, in a powerful voice that belied his wretched physical state, declared: "*Maiori forsan cum timore sententiam in me fertis quam ego accipiam*"—Perhaps your fear in passing this sentence upon me is greater than mine in accepting it.

With that, the prisoner was bundled away roughly and flung back into his airless, pitch-black cell, little more than a six-foot-square hole, in which he had spent most of the past seven years. His feet were chained to a ring in the stone floor, and the only sounds were the trickle of ice-cold water running down the walls and the scrape of scurrying rats.

In the long dark hours, hours that had pooled to days and turned to years, Giordano Bruno must have thought very deeply about what he was doing, even who he was, what he stood for. He had not seen himself as anti-Catholic but had believed he could "convert" his jailers, even convince the pope of his ideas. At least in the beginning he had believed this was possible. He had traveled throughout Europe learning and teaching. He had dabbled with Calvinism; had investigated Luther's doctrine and found much of it lacking. He had studied the teachings of the ancients, and found light and substance in the most ancient pre-Christian ideologies and faiths. He had stumbled upon Copernican thought and carried out his own thought experiments, taking Copernicus much further than the Polish monk would have conceived possible. Bruno had reached the conclusion that the universe was infinite, that there could be no personal God, ideas that half a century later would become the cornerstone to Spinoza's pantheistic, radically anticlerical theology. And Bruno had seen that in this infinite universe, there must be infinite worlds, infinite diversity, infinite possibility. All of this was anathema to the Inquisition and the Holy Office, which cherished conformity, orthodoxy, obedience.

Giordano Bruno had been born in the village of Nola, at the foot of Vesuvius. His father, Gioan, had been a professional soldier, and his mother a woman of the lower gentry named Fraulissa Salvolini. He had been considered a bright and often precocious child, and so when he reached the age of fifteen, it was decided that he should be sent to the local monastery, the Monastery of St. Domenico near Naples, to train for the priesthood.

As a youth, he had clear intentions of leading a conventional life, one spent teaching and praying, but as he grew older, the ideas of the strict Dominican doctrine and his own idiosyncratic beliefs had begun to diverge rapidly. He had accepted ordination but was never able to contain his thoughts, to preserve in silence his heterodox beliefs. Within weeks of entering the priesthood, Bruno had aroused first the suspicion and then the anger and censure of his superiors at the monastery. Unwisely perhaps, he had argued with his colleagues over the philosophy of Aristotle, attempting to expose the many inconsistencies he saw in it. He had then begun to subtly question the doctrine of the Trinity. To add insult to injury, he had gone on to write a satirical story called *Noah's Ark* which made oblique but mocking reference to unthinking believers. Worse still, he had claimed that perhaps some of those the Church branded as heretics, those who expressed religious opinions outside the circumscription of the Holy Bible, were perhaps not all ignorant, not all condemned to the flames of Hell. He had even claimed an interest in the heresy of Arianism, a faith in which the Trinity is viewed as a human fabrication and Christ considered the first "creation" of God rather than an integral aspect of the divine.

But what had sealed his fate and made Bruno a pariah at the monastery was the revelation that he had read banned texts, works of mystics and alchemists. A fellow monk (Bruno never discovered his identity) had reported him. He had been caught reading Erasmus in the privy, an offense considered so grave that the prior, Ambrogio Pasque, long tired of his errant ward, had shown no hesitation in reporting him to the provincial father to answer charges of heresy, a crime that brought with it the punishment of excommunication and, in some extreme cases, death by fire.

By this time Bruno had become quite aware that the monastic life was not for him. He was known to be an exceptionally talented intellectual with the gift of eloquence; even the prior could not deny that. But it was obvious Bruno was dangerously clever, a subversive best disposed of. And knowing how the net would have closed to entrap him, Bruno had chosen to take flight rather than face the local inquisitor. Yet, such a decision meant he was forced to begin a life without a home. He could never settle in one place for long, never feel secure. Within months he was excommunicated *in absentia,* a fugitive looking to his future but perpetually on his guard.[4]

Bruno's character, and in particular his insistence upon intellectual freedom, made him a perfect man of his time. But because of his radical views he would remain in conflict with the Church for the rest of his life. For like Galileo after him, Bruno had been born in the wrong place at the wrong time to pass unscathed through life proselytizing what was considered by most to be extreme heresy. If he had spent his life in northern Europe like Martin Luther, or even if he had applied more cunning as did Erasmus, he might have lived to enjoy old age. Instead, Bruno actually courted danger and controversy, confronting his enemies head-on.

He knew his ideas would almost certainly be unacceptable to the regimen of Catholicism, for the self-interest of the Vatican kept the Church rooted in dogma and obscurantism. The Church preached that the Eucharist involved the actual physical and spiritual communion of God with the faithful; Bruno saw it as a ritual that unified aspects of God. In his pantheistic philosophy, the faithful were themselves God; the bread and the wine elements of

---

4. It has been argued that the prior had threatened Bruno with the local Inquisitor merely to scare him, simply in an attempt to steer him toward righteousness before he went too far with his heretical ideas (Richard Westfall, Galileo@ rice.edu, Albert Van Helden, 1995). If this is true, Bruno may have overreacted by fleeing the monastery when he did—an act that did spark the anger of the Church. However, Bruno's ideologies would never have allowed him to settle into the role of the conventional priest and his unorthodox views marked him out as someone who would forever clash with official doctrine, so if he had not left then he would have done so some time later.

the divine. The Church held Aristotle's ideas to be the only true description of the physical world; Bruno found joy in ripping apart Greek philosophy and exposing its obvious inconsistencies. The Church saw itself as the one true faith; Bruno spent his entire life building a philosophy that amalgamated Catholicism with rationalism, Hermeticism, and ancient religions. The Church utterly rejected the occult (yet burned witches and exposed alchemists as heretics); Bruno used occult ideologies as one of many ways to reveal Truth, and thus to reach enlightenment. The Church wished to obfuscate, to dominate, to suppress dangerous truths, and to reveal to the faithful only the doctrinal essentials; Bruno called for freedom of information and the open exchange of learning—he embraced change, debate, and free thought.

Realizing as he did that the radical divisions between his views and the orthodox line were almost insurmountable, Bruno surely knew the flames awaited him, yet he stuck by his principles. A generation later, Galileo, for his own complex reasons, did recant and saved himself from the torch. But Bruno resisted, and if he flinched emotionally, he did not show it. However, Bruno was no madman rushing to the stake buoyed up by religious fervor; he was a rational man, a sage, a philosopher, and he understood what he was doing. And yet, to face a most terrible death at the stake with reasoned purpose, defiant and unbowed, takes a special courage, a superhuman will, a dedication almost impossible for us to imagine.

· II ·

RELIGION

And of our infirmities the most savage is to despise our being.

—Michel de Montaigne

B RUNO'S LIFE WAS circumscribed by the last half of the sixteenth century, a period often identified as the end of the Renaissance. But actually, historians have some trouble finding a consensus on the dates that mark the start and the end of this reawakening of Western culture; some would place the end of the Renaissance perhaps less than a century before the first bloom of the Enlightenment, which was germinated by the ideas of Newton, Descartes, and Locke during the late seventeenth century. But by any definition the late Renaissance may be viewed as a time during which the world was in a state of unprecedented flux. The shackles of medievalism remained, most especially in any place in which the Church was cherished, but the work of thousands of driven, passionate individuals struggling for some two centuries had, by Bruno's adulthood, given civilization a momentum that was becoming unstoppable, a forward-looking thirst for adventure, innovation, and new horizons.

Around the end of the fourteenth century, some century and a half before Bruno's birth, a small group of well-heeled Europeans seeking novelty and knowledge and (it must not be ignored) coveting prestige and social kudos actively sought out the literary and philosophical treasures of the ancients. Emissaries were sent far and wide to find lost manuscripts, Latin originals written by the semimythical figures of classical times.

The focus of all this activity was Florence, where the Medici and other wealthy noblemen nurtured a genuine appetite for knowledge and had the money and social impetus to pursue the often-distant echoes of learning. What they collected came directly from Arabic and Turkish castles, obscure monasteries and ancient decaying libraries, treasures unearthed by handpicked historians and linguists in their pay.

Some of the earliest classical Latin texts were found by Giovanni Boccaccio, Coluccio Salutati, and Giovanni Conversini. They brought to Florence a raft of important works, including Tacitus's *Histories,* Manilius's *Astronomica,* and Cicero's inflammatory *Brutus.* Then a short time later, Italian scholars (of whom Francesco Petrarch was preeminent) learned of a still older source for the ideas they had gleaned from Rome, and so the original ancient Greek manuscripts were slowly unearthed and taken to Italy, primarily to Florence. By the 1420s, hundreds of texts lay in the hands of a few wealthy patrons and the job of translating these seminal works was begun. In this way the teachings of Aristotle, Plato, Pythagoras, Euclid, Hippocrates, and Galen in their original form sparked a new era of humanism and reform along with a surge of interest in science, medicine, and philosophy.

But the Renaissance, what Engels called "the greatest progressive revolution that mankind has so far experienced," was not energized only by the past.[1] All the key figures of the period, from Leonardo to Machiavelli, were in one aspect creatures of a bygone age, infused with the ideals and thought systems of medieval Europe; but from the mid-fifteenth century (the "High Renaissance") on, such pioneers lived in a world possessed of the greatest single creation of humanity. Exactly a century before Bruno was born, Gutenberg pioneered the use of movable type and printing became practical. Gutenberg's famous forty-two-line Bible was produced around 1455; within three years there was a press in Strasbourg; twenty-five years later, in 1480, there were more than a dozen printers working in Rome; and by the end of the fifteenth century an estimated one hundred printers were toiling in Venice. By then some forty thousand titles had appeared in print. A century before Bruno's birth there had been fewer than thirty thousand books in existence, all written by hand; by the time he was teaching and traveling throughout Europe during the late sixteenth century there was already a canon of some fifty million printed books.

This was fine for intellectual progress, but in almost all mundane ways the world of 1600 was little different from that of 1450. The average life expectancy was twenty-four years for a woman and perhaps twenty-seven years for a man. The majority of people

---

1. Friedrich Engels, *Dialectics of Nature*.

were hungry and ill most of the time, and the rich suffered most of the same horrors as the poor; plague, war, and pestilence were supremely democratic. All but a few were illiterate and innumerate and spent most of their time inebriated. Most people traveled no farther than ten miles from their own homes during their entire lives and were pathologically suspicious of strangers; most had no inkling of the year in which they lived, nor knew anything of the world beyond their village or town. Their religion, although outwardly Catholic, was composed of nine parts superstition and earth magic to one part Matthew, Mark, Luke, and John; the form of Christianity they were force-fed was barely understood, enwrapped as it was in quasi-mystical terminology. Most important, the populace received its religious indoctrination in an ancient and for most people quite unintelligible language, Latin. For the fourteenth-century peasant, religious education derived solely from the Bible and orthodox sacred works was a largely meaningless affair.

For such people, everyday life was an agony and the society in which they lived was almost stagnant. Medics bled and smothered with leeches, and alchemists in their thousands nurtured avaricious dreams of transmuting base metal into gold. The waking world was controlled by bacteria carried by rats repeatedly laying waste to great swathes of the population of Europe and by wars of men that took a terrible toll on the peasant population. Meanwhile, the power of fantasy and fear fueled nightmares in which demons from an underworld stalked and slaughtered the unwary. Things started to change only with the advent of the Industrial

Revolution, around 1780, almost two centuries after the murder of Bruno.

Considerable responsibility for this sluggish progress must be laid at the door of one of the great institutions that had thrived at the core of Western civilization for some thirteen hundred years, the Christian Church. For if the secular, humanist intellectual effort of the Renaissance represents human thought in the ascendant, the Christian Church, and in particular iniquitous Catholicism, was its evil twin, heading in precisely the opposite direction.

The philosophers of the Renaissance were nearly all faithful Catholics who for the most part kept their more radical thoughts to themselves. If they did publish, as Bruno did fearlessly, their work was read only by an elite few. The Roman Church muzzled the public expression of radical views with an abiding energy and hunted down the authors of any anti-Catholic philosophies. Although they supported the proliferation of sanctioned theological knowledge among the privileged, educated classes, in a broader sense the Church leaders were instinctively anti-intellectual and deliberately obscurantist. For the cardinals jealously guarding their privileged earthly existence, the less the laity knew, the better.

Few would doubt that the Christian faith had begun with purity, but human desire quickly tainted the institution. By Bruno's time, the Church had long since sunk into a mire of corruption. But beyond this, the doctrine supplied by the Church's founding fathers provided a template for living only a very simple life. This was fine for the largely illiterate laity but quite inadequate for an inquisitive elite. As philosophers began to probe more deeply and inductive "science" superseded deductive reasoning, it became clear that orthodoxy provided inadequate models and paradigms that left more questions than answers. By the late Renaissance, the intellectually curious were finding it difficult to reconcile what was clearly observable and quantifiable with the ancient theology offered by the Church. But this incompatibility between the thinkers of the late Renaissance and orthodox Christian theologians had its roots in ancient times; indeed, the conflict extended back to the earliest days of Christian predominance.

In A.D. 325, Emperor Constantine, the leader of Western civilization, found himself overwhelmed with theological conflict, burdened by questions of doctrine, and facing one of the greatest challenges to his rule. The cause of this was a simple one. The written doctrine of the Christian faith had provided a template for the establishment of the Church and had enabled Christian leaders to found the basics of a new society within the extremely fragile political environment created by Rome's rapid decline. But the Church's bishops, extremely powerful men in this new Christian world, were fighting among themselves over some of the most basic tenets of the faith, matters that were not clear-cut in the Gospels, nor adequately settled within the sacred texts of the faith. And in this unstable world, matters of religious doctrine could prove incendiary, could unleash a global firestorm that would consume emperors, kings and popes indiscriminately.

So, in an effort to maintain his grip on the political and religious fabric of his time, Constantine called a great meeting of the Church fathers and regional politicians with the purpose of thrashing out a prospectus for Christianity, a tightly defined doctrine that would effectively bury the difficult questions and answer the slightly easier ones. A consensus would reverse the rapidly spreading disestablishment and attract rebels to a common form of worship.

This meeting was held in the city of Nicaea in what is now Turkey and has become known as the First Council of Nicaea. It was here in A.D. 325 that many of what are seen as the fundamental tenets of the Church were fabricated and designed for men by other men standing in for God. And the matters discussed, dissected, and decided upon at Nicaea were not superficial points of order or concerned with shade or nuance; they went to the very heart of faith and the Christian religion. Included on the agenda was the need to establish a set of rules for the behavior of clergy and the elucidation of a method for calculating the date when Easter falls each year. But of the many points of doctrine resolved during long rounds of debate, the most important outcome was to influence enormously the future course of Christianity and with it the lives and ideas of many important thinkers from the fourth century to the present day. The members of the council decided nothing less than the true nature of the Lord God, Creator of the Universe.

In an attempt to produce a comprehensible vision of God, they wrote their own theology, one that was both detailed and readily visualized by the uneducated. This doctrine, the concept of the Holy Trinity, was composed and voted for within the council chambers of Nicaea. To the theologians, this was seen as necessary in order to rationalize a form for the Faith and to manufacture a coherent expression of the diverse affirmations about God, all of which played an equal role in any statement of Christian experience and belief. And so it was decided that the one God was Father, Son, and Holy Spirit. The Father, or "sovereign," transcends all finite limits and is immortal and omnipotent. Jesus Christ became hugely more important than a mere prophet commissioned by God and was elevated to the stature of "the Son of God," or "the Word made flesh," divinity incarnate. The third element, the Holy Spirit, represents the divine spark in all believers; it is another way of expressing faith or holiness. For the Catholic, the Eucharist becomes a genuine transubstantiation in which the very flesh and blood of Jesus is consumed.

This radical position became known as the doctrine of *homoousios* ("of one substance") and was generated entirely from the pseudo-intellectual argument of fourth-century theologians desperate for a definition of God. But for Constantine, the head of the Council of Nicaea, there were other matters also at stake. He needed a tidy definition for the sake of political expediency, because the vexed question of the nature of God had lain at the heart of the dispute among his bishops. In one camp stood the thirty-year-old bishop of Alexandria, Athanasius, renowned author of *On the Incarnation of the Word* (c. A.D. 318) who proselytized orthodoxy. Of a very different opinion was Arius, a rebel Alexandrian priest then in his seventy-seventh year.

Arius had created the sect of Arianism around the doctrine of *homoiousios* ("of like substance"). Arians rejected the notion that Christ was of the same substance as God, and declared that the incarnation of Jesus was not an aspect of God but that the Son, while divine and like God ("of like substance"), had been created by God. Arius said of Jesus Christ that "there was a time when he was not."[2]

Constantine, always more a politician than in any sense a religious pedagogue, allowed the council to resolve in favor of Athanasius and his doctrine of *homoousios* ("of one substance"). Henceforth, Arianism was deemed to contradict official Christian teaching. Many ignored this decision, and indeed Arianism thrived during the first two centuries after the Council of Nicaea. But by the sixth century, believers were marginalized and persecuted almost to the point of extinction, and Arianism went underground and was soon perceived by Catholics as the greatest doctrinal heresy.[3]

But although its decisions were reached merely by a vote among bishops (who would have claimed their choice was divinely inspired), the Council of Nicaea did achieve what it had been designed to do; it both established a *modus operandi* for the Christian Church and resolved the greatest theological problem of the time. By the end of the fourth century, the working system for the faith had become very simple: increase power, influence, and wealth at the expense of rival ideologies, extinguish all competi-

---

2. In reference to this clash of ideologies, Edward Gibbon, the author of *The History of the Decline and Fall of the Roman Empire* (one of the titles in the Vatican's *Index Librorum Prohibitorum*), wrote with unguarded cynicism that at Nicaea, Christianity had been split over a single iota.

3. The sect of Arianism survived long after the Catholic Church tried to obliterate it. One of the most famous of Arius's followers was Sir Isaac Newton.

tion or rebellion as soon as it made itself known; and if the Gospels provided no ready model for dealing with change, be creative and indoctrinate.

Throughout the medieval period, the Church of Rome became increasingly political and worldly, merging the spiritual with the secular so that the pope became as much a head of a sovereign state as a spiritual leader. To finance papal ambitions, the Church unstintingly compromised theology, and when its manufactured doctrine proved inadequate, the cardinals stretched interpretation of the Scriptures to the breaking point.

Perhaps the most blatant expression of this was the increasing use of "indulgences" to raise money for the papal coffers. Via the system of indulgences, sinners could pay for absolution of their sins, and successive popes perverted the process so much that by the time of the Reformation this simple trick provided a major source of revenue for the Vatican. One Dominican friar, Johann Tetzel, was a sort of P. T. Barnum of his day and traveled Europe selling indulgences to the populace from a stool set up in each town square he visited. He even sold indulgences absolving sins before they had been committed. By this contrivance, a murderer could gain absolution before committing the act.

And not all the money acquired from this trade (which ran into many millions of sovereigns) was used to finance the political aspirations of popes; much of this "sinner's gold" replenished the papal coffers drained by the expense of orgiastic feasts, rare spices, fine silks, and the services of specialist prostitutes. Thus the indulgences of the pope and his favored cardinals in Rome were paid for by the indulgences of the peasantry, the whole sorry show apparently sanctioned by God.

As such wild hypocrisy escalated, Erasmus, a deeply sincere Catholic academic who yearned for papal purity, wrote a series of scathing, erudite attacks upon the clergy and highlighted the clear disparity between "Truth" and official doctrine. His *Moriae encomium* (1509; *The Praise of Folly*), a book he wrote in England while staying with his friend Thomas More, staggered Rome with his open attacks against the pope, Julius II. But what cut deepest was the fact that *Moriae encomium* was such a popular book it was rapidly translated into no fewer than a dozen languages. This represented a terrible danger to Rome simply because the Holy See had sustained itself for so long by maintaining almost total ignorance among the laity. All religious texts, including the Bible and the prayer book, were available only in Latin; all religious services and all decrees were delivered only in Latin. This meant that the vast majority of people had no idea what they were reciting in church or what they were committing their faith to. Suddenly, within Erasmus's prose difficult questions were posed in the vernacular and with them suspicion toward all levels of the clergy began to ripen just as the cardinals had feared it would. Spurred on by intellectuals like Erasmus and lower clergy in the know (men like Luther and Calvin), the laity began to question the Church and to demand clarification.

However, as radical as he was, Erasmus remained devoted to the essence of Catholicism (just as Bruno would), but the German Martin Luther thought and acted in a very different way. And when he struck, the Church was caught so wrong-footed it almost toppled. Grown lazy and overconfident, the papacy kept a wary eye on intellectual troublemakers but believed it could always effectively quash rebellion with little effort. So, even when Luther pinned his Ninety-five Theses to the door of the Castle Church in Wittenberg on October 31, 1517, Julius's successor still took no notice.[4]

By 1517, Julius had been in his tomb four years and Leo X, the second son of Lorenzo de' Medici, was on the papal throne. More concerned with his own pleasures and the continued prosperity of the Medici family, he too ignored the growing tensions. This complacency even survived the sack of Rome by the Teutonic hordes in 1527, and it was not until Paul III became pope in 1534 that the Church finally began to realize the danger it faced, and reacted.

To counter Luther's Reformation spreading through northern Europe and the increasingly vicious antipapal stance of the English monarch Henry VIII, the Church took dramatic measures. In an attempt to reeducate the masses in the style of papal choosing, the Society of Jesus, or Jesuits, was formed by Ignatius Loyola in 1534. The Council of Trent was created a few years later, in 1545, and met at irregular intervals to formulate papal policy

---

4. Yet such was Erasmus's popularity that the Church failed initially to suppress his masterpiece, *Moriae encomium*. However, at the height of the Counter Reformation the Inquisition began collecting material that might incriminate the great humanist author, an effort that continued even after he was dead. In 1544, eight years after Erasmus had died, the zealous Pope Paul IV took the extraordinary step of excommunicating him posthumously and then consigned all his works to the *Index Expurgatorius*.

designed to fend off theological attacks. It was this gathering of the upper echelons of the Church hierarchy that was to commit Galileo to trial almost a century later and, through its actions, lead Europe into the worst religious conflagration in its history, the Thirty Years War, which began in 1618.

But perhaps the most controversial policy decision made to counter the growing tide of Protestantism, scientific thought, and heresy was the creation of the Roman Inquisition, established by Pope Paul III in 1542. Modeled upon the Papal Inquisition, which had been doing its bloody work since the thirteenth century, the Roman Inquisition had as its sole aim the search for and eradication of all serious opposition to the Catholic Church, in whatever form it was found. Its official duty was to investigate and to reeducate, to bring lost souls back to the Mother Church; but in reality, the Inquisition was a weapon of revenge, a mechanism for murder, a sixteenth-century *Schutzstaffel*. This organization exterminated in excess of one million men, women, and children (one out of every two hundred people on earth at that time). Typical of this group was the Inquisitor Conrad Tors, who once declared, "I would burn a hundred innocents if there was one guilty among them."

The original Inquisition, the Papal Inquisition established by Pope Gregory IX in 1231, had been aimed at liquidating the Albigensians (or Cathars), a sect who believed in the dualistic nature of existence, abhorred all physical life, denied the concepts of Hell and Purgatory, and refuted many of the basic tenets of Catholicism. Gregory had justified the methods of the Inquisition (including physical abuse and imprisonment) by calling upon the

Augustinian interpretation of Luke 14, verse 23, which suggested that physical violence could be employed against known heretics.[5]

The Inquisition had flourished in Spain while falling into disfavor in early Renaissance Italy, but as the Reformation began to bite, Paul III decided to resurrect the ancient institution. He gave it fresh and increasingly draconian powers, and he again liberally stretched interpretation of the Scriptures to excuse a range of punishments, including confiscation of all lands and possessions, life imprisonment in solitary confinement, and almost any variety of mental and physical cruelty.

Groups of trained investigators traveled the kingdoms of Europe to unearth information about suspected heretics. Fear would precede them, and they employed subtle psychological techniques to increase this fear. In the days before their arrival, notices were posted announcing the impending visit. The Inquisitor would enter the town in a solemn procession of hooded monks. Spies had already identified anyone with heretical leanings, and these people would be rounded up to appear before the Inquisitor. With this example as a warning, the local populace were invited to confess their sins before they could be exposed by a secret source, and they were actively encouraged to report anyone they suspected of heresy. If a transgressor could bring in a dozen suspects, his own sins would be excused and he would be spared the stake.

---

5. The original verse is innocent enough. Luke declared, "And the Lord said unto the servant, go out into the highways and hedges and compel them to come in, that my house may be filled."

According to surviving manuals written by one of the most abhorrent Inquisitor Generals, Bernard Gui, the Inquisition had two forms of general citation, the *inquisitio generalis* and the *inquisitio specialis*.[6] The former was conducted in towns and cities and involved large numbers of heretics, sometimes entire populations; the *inquisitio specialis* was directed at individuals who had come to the attention of the Holy Office. Each was used pitilessly.

All that was required to bring a charge of heresy was the testimony of two informants. The suspect was imprisoned while under questioning and the Inquisition was never in a hurry. Many innocent victims died while incarcerated waiting for the Inquisitor to assess their confessions. Others were tortured to death desperate to confess to crimes of which they were actually innocent and about which they knew nothing. The informants were never identified and the statements they had made concerning the suspect were never revealed, so the accused had no information against which to defend themselves. Suspects were not allowed lawyers, and most insidious of all, the proceedings of the Inquisition were conducted in total secrecy; often the victims would simply disappear.

Of course, such despotism had a dramatic effect upon the political and social framework of the Western world. A particularly graphic illustration of this comes from the 150 years between 1500 and 1650 during which an estimated thirty thousand women (and several hundred men and children) were murdered by the

---

6. The most important of the manuals was *The Practice of Inquisition*, completed by Gui in 1324.

Inquisition. Their crime was really no crime at all, merely bad luck. They had been suspected of practicing witchcraft; bitter irony indeed, for officially, the Church rejected the notion of the occult, yet it condoned the murder of those suspected of being witches.[7]

But the Church's obsession with witchcraft caused it immeasurable harm, because while the Inquisition busied itself with hunting down and burning innocent women across Europe, Martin Luther was overlooked as he undermined the Church at its roots.

However, Luther's powerful and hugely successful rebellion did little for the fortunes of the heretic. The Protestant sects that turned so many away from Rome were in most ways no better than the Catholics. Like their papist cousins, Lutheran and Calvinist leaders were driven by self-interest and self-delusion, and they too indulged themselves in orgies of violence and persecution. One of their most famous victims was the remarkably talented medic Michael Servetus, who held dangerously outspoken religious views. He expressed these ideas in his *De trinitatis erroribus* (*On the Errors of the Trinity*) of 1531, a treatise that bluntly called for the abandonment of the cherished concept of the Holy Trinity. Arrested by the Viennese Inquisition in 1553, Servetus escaped to Geneva, the center of Calvinism, where he believed he would find sanctuary.

---

7. It has long been believed that the witch trials and the murder of so many innocents was only superficially a matter of the righteous believing they were fighting an evil force disguised as scores of thousands of witches. It is now believed this horrendous process was an example of unparalleled misogyny energized by a few powerful men within the Church hierarchy.

His belief was terribly misplaced. Calvin, who held no official public office in Geneva but was considered the city's spiritual leader, had heard of Servetus. He knew of his erudition and accomplishments in the field of medicine and a decade earlier he had been sent a draft of *De trinitatis erroribus* by Servetus himself. But Calvin had no more liking for Servetus's religious views than did the Catholics of Vienna. Instead of offering the man sanctuary, Calvin had him arrested, tried as a heretic, and sentenced to death. His execution is said to have involved a slow roasting on a spit that took two hours to kill him.[8]

But such cruelty was only one aspect of the way extreme religious zeal could become a destructive force. Extremists of all denominations murdered their fellow countrymen, and religious inflexibility and paranoia propelled entire nations toward violent struggle, rebellion, and ultimately war. As the Protestant religion became all-powerful in Germany, the rebellion of persecuted Protestant minorities in Catholic states escalated into all-out war.

Beginning in 1562, when Bruno was fourteen, a set of civil wars in France known as the Wars of Religion erupted into a European conflict lasting some thirty-five years and drew in German Protestants as well as Catholics from Italy and Spain. In Paris and other major cities, the French Calvinists, known as Huguenots, claimed persecution at the hands of the Catholic majority and organized themselves into a powerful political group. The friction between

---

8. Such an infamous act was made worse by the fact that at the time of his arrest, Servetus was on the verge of discovering the method by which blood circulates through the body, work that was some seventy-five years ahead of William Harvey's breakthrough research published in *On the Motions of the Heart and Blood* (1628).

Huguenots and Catholics then sparked the tinder of the weak French monarchy. First Charles IX (who reigned 1560–74) and then his successor, Henry III (who was murdered by a religious fanatic in 1589), faced a succession of violent Huguenot uprisings supported by foreign Protestant armies. This conflict reached a bloody climax in the St. Bartholomew's Day Massacre of August 24, 1572, when during the course of three days some seventy thousand Protestants were slaughtered. After this, a group of moderate Catholics known as the Politiques came to political prominence through the powerful Montmorency family. But they were superseded by a rabidly anti-Protestant noble family, the House of Guise, who created a group calling itself the Holy League that was violently opposed to any form of peaceful settlement with the Huguenots.

In 1589, when Bruno was living in Germany, a Guise organized the murder of Henry III (a former patron and friend of Bruno's), an action that served only to worsen the political turmoil and to escalate the violence for almost a decade. Indeed, it was not until 1598, as Bruno lay isolated from the world chained to the floor in an Inquisition prison, that a semblance of order was regained. Henry III's determined and courageous successor, Henry IV, created the Edict of Nantes, which declared liberty of conscience and equality of legal and educational rights for French Protestants and allowed them to hold government office.

But religious conflict is recrudescent. Across the world, a faith corrupted continues to breed agony, so that the account sheet remains impossible to balance. In one column, religious devotion has given us glorious works that nourish and elevate. We are enriched by the works of Giotto, Dante, Titian, Michelangelo, Milton, Palestrina, and Mozart. But we must also consider the debit column: the witch-hunts, the horrors of the Inquisition, wars of religion, bombs in Northern Ireland, the dead children of Palestine. From the mouths of the apostles spilled forth the words of the gospels offering religious ecstasy, but generations of men perverted these words and generated a fervor that to this day stifles, suffocates, and immolates.

The Wars of Religion provided a harsh backdrop to Bruno's entire adult life and added further turmoil to the usual privations and struggles of sixteenth-century common folk. Wherever Bruno traveled within Europe, doctrinal intolerance and endemic slaughter in the name of God reassured him that only a spiritual and intellectual revolution could ever disassociate religion from murder, horror, and endless pain. Holding such views, Bruno was bound to make himself an enemy of the Church; he was, without doubt, a dangerous man. Even more important than his radical theories, he threatened the Church because he represented freedom of thought, freedom of expression, and freedom of imagination—a liberalism detested and feared by Rome.

And, observing Bruno's movements from afar, following the course of his career, the Inquisitors oiled their racks and stoked their fires waiting for their prey to make a false move, waiting for the day he would fall into their hands and step into a shadowland from which he had no chance of escape. He did not disappoint them.

· III ·

VENICE

To think is to speculate with images.

—Giordano Bruno

VENICE AS BRUNO found it in 1591 was a city only just awoken from a series of political and natural upheavals. Fourteen years earlier, the plague had killed almost one-third of the population, including one of its most famous sons, the artist Titian. The people of Venice had seen four doges come and go during a mere one and a half decades, and the state was treading a delicate path acting as broker between the great powers of Europe—France, Spain, and Rome.

Positioned uniquely so that it gained cultural influence from the East, it cherished a long tradition of learning and was a cross-roads for the adventurous traveler. Marco Polo set forth from Venice in 1271, and what he and other explorers took with them as emblems of Western culture was more than matched by the knowledge and influence that flowed from east to west and passed through San Marco and the Lido. During the thousand years Venice had maintained global prominence, such learning had altered the very look of the city and created a backdrop of cosmopolitanism and liberalism. Uniquely for sixteenth-century Europe, Venice was governed by a twenty-six-member *collegio* selected by means of a primitive form of democracy. Senators came exclusively from the wealthiest families (not necessarily the most ancient or noble), but the system contained sophisticated safeguards against the obvious corruption that endangered less enlightened states. A Council of Ten composed exclusively of noblemen acted as a form of "second house" to the *collegio*.

By the sixteenth century, Venice had gloried in centuries of successful trade and had established itself as a world military power. A constant feature of this position for some six hundred years had been its disputes with the Turks, the Ottoman Empire. Venice was a Christian state and had contributed to Crusade after Crusade, but it was motivated as much by money as by God, and through its struggles with the Ottoman Empire as well as with its European neighbors, it had sought always to expand its territories. Success and wealth had added splendor and beauty to an already glorious city-state. Between 1588 and 1591, the year of Bruno's arrival in Venice, the aptly named Ponte brothers had constructed the Rialto Bridge as we see it today, and during the second half of the sixteenth century the accommodations of the Doges' Palace were expanded enormously to include new prisons, apartments, and government offices.

In its relations with Rome, at the border where Venice's interest in money clashed with the faith of her people, the city's rulers inevitably walked a delicate tightrope. Successive popes had clashed with successive doges, and efforts to compromise were often exhausting and expensive for everyone. The Edict of Nantes had placed huge stress on the political stability of Europe, appeasing the Protestants and some of the Catholics in France, but making Pope Clement VIII a very nervous man. Within this atmosphere of uncertainty, Venice and Rome squabbled over disputed territories, but these were less significant than painful clashes over doctrine and ideological independence. The pope was ever suspicious that Venice had become a happy hunting ground for a motley assortment of Calvinists, Lutherans, occultists, and other heretics. More often than not, behind the scenes, diplomats smoothed arguments and each state awarded concessions to the other to avoid open conflict; it was in everyone's interest to effect a compromise whenever possible. Sometimes Venice won a dispute, sometimes Rome. Clement made it forcefully clear that the Holy See was the spiritual guide of Venice, but the Venetian government won the right to allow its booksellers to trade in books on the *Index Librorum Prohibitorum*. The pope insisted the state finance the building of more churches; the Venetians gained the right to allow Calvinist literature to be freely published and distributed in the city. Such compromise allowed the Venetians to make a living and to reserve their plot in the world to come, while the pope kept face and felt secure about his Venetian charges.

Consequently, Venice was the most liberal southern European state and welcomed unorthodox philosophers. The Venetians had also long remained distrustful of the Inquisition. For some fifty years after Pope Gregory IX had first founded the Inquisition in 1231, successive Venetian governments had refused even to allow

Inquisition administrators to set foot in the city. This decision was reversed only when, in 1288, Pope Nicholas IV threatened the Venetian ruler, Doge Giovanni Dandolo, with excommunication unless he complied with the Vatican's wishes. Even then, the Venetian Inquisitors remained disinterested in mirroring the rabid enthusiasm of their Roman counterparts. As late as 1521, during the height of the Reformation, Venice quietly defied papal orders. It established its own Inquisition rules, which dictated that all trials must be conducted by two bishops and torture in any form was banned. For forty-two years, between 1552 and 1594, just 150 trials were held in which Venetian citizens were accused of magical incantation, witchcraft, and sorcery, and just six of these led to prosecution. Throughout the ignominious century and a half of the witch-hunts, not a single person was executed or severely tortured in Venice.

Such independence of spirit had chafed relations between Venice and Rome. When King Henry III of France was assassinated, Venice gave political asylum to his rightful successor, the Protestant sympathizer Henry of Navarre. This had incensed the zealous House of Guise, angered Philip of Spain, and infuriated Pope Sixtus V to the point where he considered excommunicating the entire state of Venice. Sixtus stayed his hand only after sensibly taking the advice of trusted cardinals who pointed out that in the past the weapon of excommunicating Venice had merely energized revolt. The city had been struck by the ultimate papal threat three times during its history, by Martin IV in 1284, by Clement V in 1309, and most recently by Pope Sixtus IV in 1483, and each time the Vatican had been forced to back down and reinstate

Venice to the faith. The Venetian people would be forever influenced as much by worldly pursuits as by any religious sentiment. And it was upon this finely balanced relationship that Bruno's fate was to turn.

⚬⚬⚬

Bruno had been invited to Venice in 1591 by a nobleman named Giovanni Mocenigo. Mocenigo's first letter to Bruno was sent while the magus was in Frankfurt working to promote his latest work, *De immenso,* the first part of a trilogy in which he attempted to link together the many aspects of his cosmological and religious thinking. Mocenigo had heard of Bruno through contacts in Germany, where he had done business with a number of publishers. During the spring and summer of 1591, he sent Bruno a series of letters in which he expressed a keen interest in the philosopher's work and asked him to travel to Venice in order to tutor him in the philosophy he espoused. With each letter, Mocenigo had grown increasingly persuasive, offering Bruno handsome financial rewards that increased by the page, splendid accommodations, and the opportunity to make important contacts.

According to records linked to Bruno's trial, Mocenigo was particularly interested in Bruno's studies of the art of memory, mnemonic techniques the magus had adapted from the ancients. In his correspondence with Bruno, Mocenigo claimed to have read his many books on the subject but expressed the view that he could fully develop his skills only by direct contact with the great Giordano Bruno himself; for this privilege he was willing to pay well.

Mocenigo lived in the beautiful Campo San Samuele on the

Grand Canal directly opposite the palazzo in which Robert Browning later died in 1889. He was a senator and had been born into an aristocratic Venetian family. Reported to be immensely wealthy, he is also thought to have possessed a fickle temperament, prone to adopting fleeting fascinations over which he became obsessed before dropping them without ceremony. By all accounts he was also a deceitful character, widely distrusted and disliked.

At first, Bruno did not deign to reply to Mocenigo. Some might say that given Bruno's personal history, only a madman would have taken seriously the idea of returning to Italy and exposing himself to certain arrest and prosecution; and at the moment in Frankfurt when he did choose to return to Italy, his reasons were explained to no one.

Yet, if we probe his reasoning, what do we find? Mocenigo was certainly very keen to have Bruno in Venice, and for his part, Bruno had earned very little money throughout his life, teaching and writing. The opportunity to teach in Venice and at nearby Padua, which had a reputation for encouraging wealthy students, may have added extra spice to the idea. But then, Bruno had never before shown great interest in money and had done nothing to accrue wealth even though opportunities had presented themselves to him before Mocenigo appeared on the scene.

Once Bruno was in Venice, several factors played their part in keeping him there. Most important was the sudden death of Pope Innocent IX a few weeks after Bruno arrived.[1] On February 2, 1592,

---

1. Incredibly, Rome had three popes between the death of Sixtus V in August 1590 and the accession of Clement VIII in February 1592. Urban VII reigned for just

Ippolito Aldobrandini became Pope Clement VIII. As a cardinal, Aldobrandini had gained a reputation for compassion and tolerance, and Bruno believed that now he might seek absolution from the Inquisition and remain safely in Italy.

Even so, Bruno's return horrified his associates living outside Italy, and they reacted to news of his acceptance of Mocenigo's offer with consternation and trepidation.

"Tell me," an incredulous former associate of Bruno's living in Brandenburg wrote to a friend in Padua, "it is said that Giordano Bruno the Nolan whom you knew at Wittenberg is living among you in Padua. Can this be so? What manner of man is this, an exile, as he was used to admit, to dare to reenter Italy? I marvel, I marvel, nor can I believe it, although I have it from a sure source. Tell me, is this news false or true?"[2]

It is easy to understand such consternation. Bruno was risking much, and we can only assume magnified self-confidence and an exaggerated sense of self-worth provided him with the strength he needed. He was blind to the genuine dangers and believed he would find acceptance and leniency.

There was much to attract Bruno to Venice. A generation earlier, one of the most famous men of his age, Giulio Camillo, had built in the heart of the city what he called the Memory Theater.

twelve days in September 1590; Gregory XIV for ten months, from December 1590 to October 1591; and Innocent IX for sixty-two days, from October to December of the same year. Each was elderly and found the strain of office too much.

2. Letter dated January 21, 1592, from Havekenthal of Brandenburg to Michael Forgacz of Bavaria, recorded in *Acidalius, Valens; Epistle. A fratre editum* (Frankfurt, 1606), p. 10.

Camillo, an intellectual and onetime professor of philosophy at the University of Bologna, held many views Bruno would have shared. Indeed, as soon as he arrived in Venice, Bruno began to seek out the keepers of the occult flame Camillo had carried.

Bruno had long been fascinated by the occult. During the year before his return to Italy he had been living in a castle near Zurich owned by the renowned alchemist Johan Heinrich Hainzell, who had built a laboratory there and had spent much of his wealth seeking the philosophers' stone. During his trials, Bruno denied any link with the mystical arts, but the evidence for his close associations with magic could be found in his books and through his known connections with Hermeticists such as the renowned English magus John Dee. He had also enjoyed a close personal relationship with King Henry III of France, who was obsessed with the magic tradition and for many years acted as patron of no less a figure than Nostradamus.

The most important intellectual group in Venice was the Accademia degli Uranici, which had been founded by Fabio Paolini in 1587. Paolini had published several important works, foremost of which was a treatise on memory called *Hebdomades*, published in Venice in 1589. It was not only an important cerebral work but something of a best-seller in occult circles, a text seen by many as the very embodiment of Venetian occultism. This book had greatly inspired Bruno in his own investigations into the subject.

Within a short time of arriving in Venice, Bruno had been invited to attend meetings of the Accademia degli Uranici. Here gathered not just the celebrated occultists who passed through the city and the academics drawn there from close-by Padua, but many liberal thinkers and philosophers, men of various religious persuasions, interested in the cross-fertilization of the occult and natural philosophy. One of Venice's most famous sons, Paolo Sarpi, a friend of Galileo's and a revered protoscientist, politician, and Servite priest, was a prominent member of the group and knew Bruno well.

Sometimes this circle met in secret conclave in members' homes to talk philosophy, exchange ideas that lay at the forefront of intellectual endeavor, and discuss and interpret the work of radical thinkers. One of the leading lights of the academy, the wealthy intellectual Andrea Morosini, was a particularly gracious host of such clandestine meetings, and Bruno (who was considered something of a catch by the Venetian cabalists and philosophers) was welcomed warmly.

Other important members included many of the more successful booksellers of Venice, who provided the primary source of occult and philosophical material from across Europe. Of these, the best-known was a young Sienese named Giovanni Battista (more usually known as Ciotto), who owned a bookshop called Minerva in the main Venetian thoroughfare, the Merceria. He had met Bruno at Frankfurt and was almost certainly the one who provided a link between Bruno and the Venetian occult circle. Before Bruno's arrival, Ciotto had been proselytizing Brunian ideology and selling copies of his books printed in Paris and London during the 1580s.

What was discussed behind the closed doors of these meetings will probably never be known. But as the net tightened around Bruno, his new friends did not melt away into the shadows. These characters were well used to conspiracy and the dangers that accompanied their interests. Equally, their attitude toward authority was as defiant as one might expect of such rebellious thinkers. These men walked on eggshells, and when they were later called upon to give accounts before the Inquisition concerning Bruno, they, like their enemies in the Vatican, closed ranks and protected their own; nothing was revealed, none of Bruno's secret "philosophies" admitted.

When Mocenigo initially invited Bruno to Venice, he had offered him accommodations in his luxurious palazzo, but not then willing to fall in completely with his new patron, Bruno had chosen to find his own digs. He had little money and did not want to accept charity from Mocenigo, so, soon after his arrival, Bruno began to look for a teaching position. Through his contacts in the Accademia degli Uranici he was invited to teach at the nearby University of Padua.

Founded in 1222, the university had by the second half of the sixteenth century acquired a reputation for attracting wealthy students, drawn there in equal measure by its academic record and its proximity to the pleasure palaces of Venice. It was the Italian Oxbridge of its day, and many of the great intellectual figures of the time had passed through its portals either as students or tutors. The principal secretary to Queen Elizabeth I of England, Francis Walsingham, had studied there, and in early 1592, Galileo accepted the position of professor of mathematics.

The journey from Venice is a short one. Most commuters now take the train from Ferrovia in Venice and reach the heart of

Padua in under half an hour, but a slower, more sedate route is to journey by boat. In Bruno's day this was the only fast link between the two cities. For a brief time during the last months of 1591, Bruno availed himself of a twice-daily public boat service, making the trip several times a week, until he took rooms in Padua close to the university.

Official courses at Padua were much the same as those delivered in most other universities throughout Europe. Aristotelian rhetoric remained high on the agenda, and classical learning provided the core of the curriculum. However, unusually for the time, teachers who held unorthodox views had the right to conduct private lectures in their own rooms. And although these courses were never officially sanctioned by the university, they were often well attended.

Having taught in at least half a dozen academic centers across Europe, Bruno was an experienced and confident speaker and teacher. Indeed, his eloquence was one of his most valuable talents, and he attracted fee-paying students with his idiosyncratic confection of anti-Aristotelian invective combined with his own interpretation of Copernican astronomy spiced with risqué material from the Hermetic tradition. Within weeks his lectures had become so well attended and lucrative he decided to leave Venice for a while and take up residence in Padua, with the intention of staying through Christmas and into the early spring of the following year, 1592.

It is likely that throughout his season in Padua, Bruno remained in touch with those he knew in Venice, and he is certain to have made regular trips between the two cities, checking on the progress of his books on sale in Venice and spending time with the man who had invited him to return to Italy. It seems that during the winter, Giovanni Mocenigo had begun to gain Bruno's trust, and by March 1592, Bruno decided to return to Venice and finally to accept Mocenigo's invitation to reside in his palazzo and take him on as a pupil.

And what of this man Mocenigo? We have no personal testament concerning his involvement with Bruno, because he was prevented by Inquisition rules from recording in his memoirs or even his private diaries anything pertaining to his role in Bruno's arrest and trial. All we have is his statements to the Inquisition used during the Venetian hearings. But these, as we shall see, do provide at least a little insight into his motivations and character. He was certainly devious and manipulative, but it is also clear he was in actuality little more than a pawn in the hands of greater powers.

Feigning interest in the occult, he flattered Bruno by demonstrating an avid interest in his ideas and work.[3] "Mocenigo," Bruno later told his Inquisitors, "claimed he would support me well and I should be satisfied with him."

Even a flattered and well-paid Bruno must have harbored suspicions and misgivings. But if he did, he did not show it, nor, it seems, did he listen to the warnings of his friends. They knew that prior to his earliest communication with Bruno at Frankfurt, Giovanni Mocenigo had shown precious little interest in the

---

3. Mocenigo's primary area of interest was the "art of memory" or mnemonics, which was the subject of his letters to Bruno in Frankfurt. I will deal with this arcane discipline in the following chapter.

occult, the art of memory, or any other esoteric learning. Surely, they reasoned, such sudden interest was suspect.

For two months the two men continued to circle each other. Bruno taught Mocenigo the basics of mnemonics and discussed the elements of natural philosophy, but Mocenigo always wanted more. "Mocenigo not only wished me to teach him all I know, but desired to learn what I am unable to teach anybody," Bruno told the Inquisition. "He has constantly threatened me in life and honor if I did not give him my knowledge."[4]

Mocenigo, it seems, was himself playing a dangerous multifarious game. We know that for some years he had been working for the Venetian Inquisition, and he had almost certainly cultivated close links with the Roman Inquisition, including some with senior Vatican officials who had been following Bruno's career with interest. It was these men who had encouraged Mocenigo to forge a relationship with Bruno with the deliberate intention of trapping the philosopher. In his statement to the Venetian Inquisition, Mocenigo admits this, claiming he had deliberately ensnared Bruno and had from the beginning been driven by piety.

This must have required great delicacy on Mocenigo's part, for with one false move he could have lost Bruno entirely and gravely disappointed his masters in Rome. By this time, the Roman Inquisitors may have become reliant upon Mocenigo's scheme, seeing it as their only realistic chance of capturing Bruno; and anyone living in sixteenth-century Italy would have known that

---

4. Doc. vii.

Vatican cardinals and Roman Inquisitors did not make noble enemies.

Meanwhile, Bruno was continuing to ignore the warnings of his friends. Ciotto the bookseller at least seemed aware of what was going on in Mocenigo's palazzo in the Campo San Samuele. During Bruno's trial, Ciotto told the judges that Senator Mocenigo had made no pretensions about his motives and said in confidence: "I wish to find out what I can draw from him [Bruno] of the instructions he has promised me, not to lose altogether what I have given him, and then I shall hand him over to the censure of the Holy Office."[5]

On Friday, May 22, matters finally came to a head when Bruno decided it was time he left Mocenigo's home and Venice itself. He kept his plans strictly secret; only his amanuensis Herman Besler, a German student, knew. They prepared to make their way to Padua and then proceed to Frankfurt. "I resolved to return to Frankfurt and get certain of my works printed," Bruno was to tell the Inquisition a few days later. But that evening, Mocenigo returned home unexpectedly early and found Bruno in his room with his servant folding clothes into a trunk. Besler was dismissed and the two men argued. "He [Mocenigo] insisted on my remaining," Bruno told the court, "but I was equally set on going. He began to complain that I had not taught him what I promised. Then he used threats saying he would find means, if I did not remain of my own free will, to compel me."[6] After a heated

---

5. Doc. v.
6. Doc. vi.

exchange, Bruno bought himself time by telling Mocenigo he would at least stay another night. Then Mocenigo left the room and Bruno retired to bed.

But Mocenigo's trap had already been put into place. In the early hours of the next morning, Bruno was waked by loud shouts from outside his room. Moments later, the door burst open. Mocenigo stormed in with his manservant Bartolo. The two men were accompanied by five or six burly gondoliers from the neighborhood. They dragged Bruno roughly from his bed and bundled him through a maze of alleyways to a garret room close to San Marco. The gondoliers then carried him to the top of some stairs that led to a basement and kicked him to the bottom. A few hours later, Mocenigo returned with a group of government soldiers and an arrest warrant from the Venetian Inquisition. All Bruno's possessions were confiscated and his books and manuscripts handed over to the authorities. Then he was bound and taken to the Prison of the Inquisition facing the Doges' Palace. Bruno now found himself in the hands of His Very Reverend Paternity the Father Inquisitor for Venice.

· IV ·

MYSTICISM

He who desires to philosophize must first of all doubt all
things. He must not assume a position in a debate before
he has listened to the various opinions, and considered
and compared the reasons for and against. He must never
judge or take up a position on the evidence of what he has
heard, on the opinion of the majority, the age, merits, or
prestige of the speaker concerned, but he must proceed
according to the persuasion of an organic doctrine which
adheres to real things, and to a truth that can be understood by the light of reason.

—Giordano Bruno

GIORDANO BRUNO WAS no ordinary philosopher. He was
a cerebral maverick, a misanthrope, and an extreme intellectual radical. During an age when all but a few thought no further
than acquiring their next meal and looking after their children,
Bruno was one of a tiny group who took current ideas and extrap-
olated them to new and original vistas. As was the case with many
intellectuals of his time, much of his thinking had roots in the
past, within the ideas of other intrepid philosophers. Against tradition, Bruno argued for the concept of an infinite universe, which
he visualized as filled with inhabited worlds. He claimed all matter

was intimately linked to all other matter, that we live in a universe in which everything is recycled, all things are related; a universe in which we are in God, and God is in us. But even when his thoughts traveled to the limits of accepted reason, he retained a genuine commitment to many of the fundamentals of Christian doctrine. He loathed what the Church had become, but loved his God.

Of course, before, during, and after Bruno's time there were others who also thought in heterodox ways. Many of Bruno's contemporaries wrote about and taught a blend of mysticism and natural philosophy. Girolamo Cardano, Bernardino Telesio, and, most notably, Tommaso Campanella all shocked the faithful and intrigued the curious with their amalgamations of philosophy with non-Christian ideologies. But what made Bruno unique was his ability to take the protoscience of his day, combine it with vast erudition and a natural empathy for the ideologies of pre-Christian religion, and teach the resultant doctrine with unparalleled gusto. This heady brew was in part a nonmathematical form of science (or natural philosophy as it was then known) and in part a spiritual doctrine. Bruno, like others before him and thousands after him, believed he could rediscover the lost *harmonia mundi*; he sought the *prisca sapientia*, the unity of all knowledge, the ultimate truth.

In this respect at least, Bruno was a man of his time. Born toward the end of the Renaissance, he was infused with the intellectual Zeitgeist, and a major element of this was the conviction among the educated elite that the *prisca sapientia* was achievable, that humanity was close to acquiring the great hidden truth that would unlock all mysteries and lead to a new golden age of understanding.

For these men, the model offered by the simplistic mechanisms of Christianity was too confining. Intellect was outgrowing faith, moving far beyond the medieval matrix.

Until this moment in history, philosophical reasoning had followed two quite independent paths. One was the route chosen by the natural philosopher, who took the ideas of Aristotle as a springboard to help define the material world. The other was the route of the occultist, chosen by men who, in strictly clandestine fashion, pursued the art of Hermes Trismegistus and the ancient magi of the pre-Christian world. Only rarely did the two avenues cross within extraordinary figures. Albertus Magnus, Roger Bacon, Thomas Aquinas, and Leonardo da Vinci were such rare conduits; for most of the time, followers striding along one path ignored and often despised those pounding the other. But like Aquinas, Bacon, and da Vinci, Bruno was one in whom the twinned intellectual routes met, although in him they reached a unique apotheosis.[1]

For reasons still not fully understood, two figures emerged

---

1. Some readers may wonder why *three* parallel paths of human intellectual development—natural philosophy, the occult tradition, and Christianity—are not listed here. The last has been ignored for one important reason. Christian doctrine does not evolve; it is based upon cast-in-stone tenets and therefore cannot develop or offer anything radical or original. Of course, both the occult avenue and the Christian heritage share the encumbrance of being faith-based thought systems, but what differentiates them markedly is that Christian theology violently rejects change or innovation, whereas the occult tradition thrived upon these things. If nothing else, this willingness to embrace intuition and inventiveness could unite the natural philosopher (or protoscientist) with the mystic or occultist, so that each eventually found that they were almost totally incompatible with theology, yet shared some fundamental concerns.

from Hellenic times as intellectual standard-bearers of their age towering above all other classical thinkers: Aristotle and Plato. Aristotle (384–322 B.C.) was the man who laid the first stone for the natural philosopher, and he dominated the prescientific path for two thousand years, providing civilization with shape and form. Yet, ironically, on almost every level and about every subject, he was utterly wrong, and the far superior ideas of other Greek thinkers were ignored and for a long time forgotten, trampled underfoot by fate and the voracious force of Aristotle's supporters.

Aristotle's work was encyclopedic in scope. He was as interested in astronomy as he was in botany, logic, or geology. His weakest subject was what later became known as physics, but ironically, it was his ideas in this discipline that had the greatest impact upon future generations. His most famous works, *On Generation and Corruption* and the *Physical Discourse*, which described his ideas concerning motion, time, matter, and the heavenly and earthly realms, were lauded as the ultimate scientific authority from the time they were written during the fourth century B.C. until the Enlightenment some twenty centuries later.

Aristotle described a model in which the observed material world is composed entirely from a blend of just four elements: fire, air, water, and earth. If these are left to settle, he argued, they arrange themselves into layers. This came from simple observations such as the fact that water falls through air (or air moves up through water in the form of bubbles) and earth (such as stones and other dense matter) falls through water and air. Fire, he then reasoned, exists in the top layer because it moves up through air. By the same token, rain falls downward because it is trying to return to its rightful place, a layer beneath air. Finally, because flames of a fire clearly rise upward, they are occupying their proper position above the other three elements. And Aristotle's ideas about the motion of objects and the nature of what later natural philosophers referred to as "forces" were equally confused. Most nebulous was his notion of the Unmoved Mover, the name he gave to the omnipotent being who he imagined maintained the movement of the heavens and kept the sun and the planets traveling about the earth.

Aristotle's ideas about astronomy were just as muddled and often unrelated to reality. He insisted that the earth was made of denser matter than what he called the "heavenly sphere." For Aristotle, the earth was an imperfect, gross realm, while the heavens and stars were made from a mysterious ethereal fifth element. From this he derived a geocentric model based upon the idea that the heavier, denser matter from which the earthly realm was formed always sought the center of the universe.[2] Finally, he proposed a simple model for a universe in which the stars are fixed in spheres and epicycles about the earth, itself fixed rigid and immutable at the center of Creation, placed there by a God who controlled all things, initiated all motion, and determined all fates. This system provided the starting point for Ptolemy (c. A.D. 100–170) some five centuries later; Ptolemy devised a geocentric world system that was the standard, accepted model for fifteen hundred years.

---

2. Aristotle was not the only ancient to propose the idea of a geocentric universe. This misconception was also offered by a contemporary of Aristotle's, Eudoxus, and again, nearly two centuries after Aristotle, by the Alexandrian Hipparchus.

As these ideas laid a path for the natural philosopher, more interesting and exciting doctrines were sidelined. Most important of these were the teachings of Democritus (460–370 B.C.), which have survived in the verses of the Roman historian Lucretius (95–55 B.C.). Writing with a breathtaking elegance, Lucretius offered a lucid description of Democritus's philosophy. "But things are formed, now, from specific seeds," he declared. "Hence each at birth comes to the coasts of light from a thing possessed of its essential atoms. Thus anything cannot spring from anything, for things are unique; their traits are theirs alone. And why in spring do we see roses, grain in summer, vines produce at autumn's call, if not because right atoms in right season have streamed together to build each thing we see."[3]

Democritus described a mechanical universe, but one very different from Aristotle's. In this model the most fundamental components of matter are atoms, and these create all movement and dynamism by their collisions with one another. Democritus and his followers were so keen on this concept that they applied "atomism" to every aspect of the observed world and went further still by attempting to explain human behavior as a consequence of atomic collisions. By thinking in this way, on an empirical level at least, Democritus was millennia ahead of his time and operated in an entirely different league from the relative amateurism of Aristotle. Democritus had no mathematical interpretation for atomism, nor any experimental support, but in essence, his conceptual model was dramatically closer to the modern model shaped by

---

3. Lucretius, "The Persistence of Atoms," from *The Nature of Things* (c. 60 B.C.).

Antoine Lavoisier and John Dalton during the late eighteenth and early nineteenth centuries. We may only wonder what ideas might have filled the minds of Renaissance natural philosophers if Democritus, rather than Aristotle, had been the voice of Hellenic "science."

The other pillar of Hellenic wisdom, Aristotle's teacher, Plato (428–348 B.C.), had been inclined to a more mystical vision of the world than his famous pupil ever was. If we think of Aristotle as stone and metal, fire and thunder, Plato is gossamer lightness and dreamy numeric juggling. In fact, to Plato, mathematics was everything. In his enthusiasm he had written over the door of his academy: "Let no man enter who knows no geometry." But he tempered this obsession with another: the conviction that humanity (rather than just the earth) lay at the center of all things. Believing the cosmos to be a single living organism with a body, a soul, and reason, Plato became the first thinker to propose that the philosopher could reach a profound understanding of God through the study of His creation, Nature. For Plato and his disciples, the investigation of the world in which we live was an imperative, the very reason we exist at all. Taking this anthropocentric line to its ultimate conclusion, Plato believed the universe had been created and was controlled by a supreme being who had a special role for humanity. Plato took this concept so far that he even suggested the planets moved as they did simply to mark the passing of time for humankind.

But, for all this wayward thinking, the kernel of a great notion lay at the heart of Platonic thought. Plato's was a dynamic, holistic vision of the universe that was an inspiration to many great intellectuals. It counterpointed the brute force of pure Aristotelianism and encouraged an acceptance of seemingly contrary ideas, thrived on the melding of opposites and sought overarching grandiose answers. One day, some two and a half thousand years after Plato, holistic thinking would again come to the fore as twenty-first-century scientists continued to seek the *prisca sapientia.* For this is precisely the ultimate goal of the particle physicists and cosmologists (such as Steven Weinberg and Stephen Hawking) who are presently struggling to create a Grand Unified Theory, a seamless blend of quantum theory, a theory of gravity, and relativity.

Aristotelianism soon became the bedrock of all rationalism, and then later, during the earliest centuries after Christ, its status was enhanced enormously in a marriage with Christian theology. Aristotelianism became the official universal model for orthodox teaching, "Church science." The scriptures defined the spiritual world; the Hellenic tradition epitomized by Aristotle's fantasy described the material. Crucially, each supported the other.

This marriage was represented best by the Scholastics, European monks of the Middle Ages who had copies of many Greek works taken from originals first seen by Europeans during the Crusades. Many of these originals had survived the repeated sacking of Alexandria and had been rescued from the flames by bounty hunters. They had been sold and resold until they reached the hands of Arabic intellectuals who translated them and used them as a basis for their own scientific studies; these translations (along with the monastery libraries of Europe) acted as one of the few repositories of human knowledge during the Dark Ages.

Together, the ideas of Aristotle in manuscript form and the words of the apostles and the Old Testament writers produced a self-contained and self-consistent image of the universe. According to this model, God had created the world precisely as the Scriptures described and He continued to guide all action. Every object had been set in motion by God and was supervised by divine power. In this way, the Church's doctrine of divine omnipotence fit neatly with Aristotelian concepts such as the Unmoved Mover.

Beyond this, orthodoxy decreed that all matter consisted of the four elements as Aristotle had stated during the fourth century B.C., and that every material object was a complete individual entity created by God, composed of varying combinations of the four elements. Each object possessed certain distinct and observable qualities, such as heaviness, color, smell, and coolness. These were seen as *solely* intrinsic aspects or properties of the object, and their observed nature had nothing to do with the perception of the observer. Orthodoxy also supported other Aristotelian beliefs long since disproved: the idea that we see things because our eyes project particles that bounce off viewed objects, and that an object moves through the air because, as it does so, the displaced air in front of it flows behind it instantaneously and pushes it onward. Most important for Bruno's fate, the line the Church took on astronomy was wholeheartedly geocentric, purely Aristotelian, and supported by Ptolemy's model.

This then was the path of natural philosophy, an often torturous journey from the almond groves of the Peloponnesus via the Arabic intellectuals and mathematicians to the ice-cold wet stone libraries of Dark Age monasteries. This learning seeped out and was adopted practically to the letter by the administrators of the great universities where clerics taught and the clerics of the next generation listened, scribbled, and, almost to a man, accepted without question.

But not everyone was fooled. A brave, maverick few began to whisper dissent; they saw obvious inconsistency and refused to accept what was, from their own experience, clearly false. These men contributed to a creeping awareness that all was not right with official doctrine or natural philosophy.

The most famous of this group of contemporaries were Thomas Aquinas (1224–74), Albertus Magnus (1200–80), and Roger Bacon (1220–92). In much of their writing, Thomas Aquinas and Albertus Magnus stuck to the traditional Classical line and maintained a firm belief that man was the central object of the Creation and that the universe was designed for him by God. In private, however, they espoused the merits of alchemy and conducted investigations into quite unorthodox areas of knowledge. They were even said to have designed an automaton that could walk and talk and behave like a man, while conducting experiments to find the *elixir vitae*.[4]

The great Oxford scholar and Franciscan Roger Bacon was more open about his researches and is now seen by many science historians as one of the first to erode the restrictions inherent in the philosophy of the Scholastics. He was the first to understand

---

4. Charles Mackay, "The Alchemysts," in *Memoirs of Extraordinary Popular Delusions,* by Richard Bentley (London, 1841), pp. 105–7.

the power of experiment, and he composed three farsighted tracts, *Opus majus, Opus minor,* and *Opus tertium,* which together outline his philosophy and his experimental techniques across a range of disciplines. Bacon's efforts gained him an esteemed place in the history of science, but in his lifetime his work was viewed as heretical and its anti-Aristotelian elements as subversive. In 1277, the anti-occultist minister-general of the Franciscans grew suspicious of Bacon's ideas, and when the English monk rather naively presented the head of his order with a special edition of his trilogy, he was thrown in jail, where he died fifteen years later.

Men like Bacon, as brilliant as they were, lived in the wrong age to do much more than dent Aristotelianism, but as the Renaissance blossomed, dissenting voices grew louder and more numerous. Leonardo da Vinci was originally a supporter of Aristotle, until he began to conduct his own experiments and to learn, as Bacon had before him, that what the Greek philosopher said about the world was in obvious conflict with experience. Leonardo wrote thousands of pages of notes in which he constantly criticized Aristotle (and took swipes at Plato), but because he kept these notes secret, nothing of his radical ideas was known during his lifetime. Upon Leonardo's death, his notes were lost for almost two hundred years, rediscovered only during the seventeenth century at the beginning of the Enlightenment. As a sad result, Bruno was totally unaware of the discoveries of his countryman, made a century before his own time.

Through such confusion and because most researchers kept their heretical ideas to themselves or were destroyed like Bacon, the world had to wait until an auspicious collision of ideas and methodology before events could conspire to change the prevailing view. And that moment came a quarter of a century after Leonardo's death and a full century and a half after Roger Bacon's slow murder. It was not until then that one man dared to throw reason and recorded observation in the face of irrationality and in so doing transformed human thought, buried Aristotle, and hacked at the foundations of Christian theology. That man was Nicolaus Copernicus.

Copernicus (1473–1543) was a Polish priest who had studied medicine at Padua and then law at the University of Ferrara, earning a doctorate in canon law in 1503. As he conducted his official studies he had, like so many great thinkers before and after him, followed a separate unorthodox path of learning. And for Copernicus, his muse was the heavens, the poetry of stellar motion, the grand procession of the planets. Unconvinced by what the masters had written, he dedicated himself to understanding the true nature of the universal dynamic, the way in which celestial bodies moved. He labored long into the night unraveling the mysteries of the heavens, while by day he toed the orthodox line.

But, as fascinated as Copernicus may have been, he was also very much aware of the dangerous nature of any thoughts leaning toward an anti-Aristotelian worldview, most especially within the sensitive area of what would one day become astronomy and cosmology. During the fifteenth century, the Church was particularly anxious to keep intellectuals away from any reinterpretation of universal mechanics. As far as the cardinals were concerned, the celestial realm—what the Greeks referred to as the "heavenly sphere"—was quite definitely off-limits; it was God's territory.

Indeed, even questioning Aristotelian totalitarianism fell afoul of a set of what were called "the 219 dangerous propositions," defined in 1227 by Bishop Stephen Tempier, someone who at least had the imagination to see the dangers of epistemology and the inquisitive nature of the human mind.

So Copernicus did what any sensible researcher of the time would do: he wrote in secret and kept his innermost thoughts strictly private. Over a period of thirty years, from 1513 until the year of his death in 1543, Copernicus gathered a vast and detailed collection of astronomical observations, all recorded and reported with only the vaguest thoughts of ever publishing the conclusions he was beginning to draw from his nightly clandestine labors.

In 1543, Copernicus fell ill and came to realize he was dying. Secretly, he arranged for his heretical papers to be printed and published. He had no close family, no one Rome could destroy after he had gone, and so he could now expose his ideas to everyone who might be interested.

His book was entitled *De revolutionibus orbium coelestium* (*On the Revolutions of the Heavenly Spheres*), and legend has it that one of the first copies to emerge from the press was placed on the author's deathbed. If this was indeed true, Copernicus must have felt deeply satisfied to learn his life's work had finally reached the press, but it was to be many years before his ideas would be widely understood and interpreted, and many more before they would be accepted.

First, Copernicus's publisher, a Lutheran minister named Andreas Osiander, had tried to head off any controversy that might embroil him by adding a preface to the book without the author's consent. In this he had declared that the treatise was not to be considered a statement of reality but merely an aid to the calculation of planetary movement. But beyond this, although the contents of *On the Revolutions of the Heavenly Spheres* were extremely radical, they were presented in a misleading and sometimes confused way. Perhaps Copernicus did this deliberately. It is possible he took his lead from the alchemists and mystics of the time and, on a superficial level at least, had attempted to dull the book's impact.

At the heart of Copernicus's theory was his observation that the stars and the planets moved in such a way that the earth could not possibly lie at the center of the universe, but in the account of these findings he had, with significant innovations, clung to many traditional Ptolemaic and Aristotelian concepts. He adhered to Aristotle's notion that the stars and planets followed perfect circular paths and that such planetary motion could be explained by means of complicated combinations of circles called epicycles, as suggested by Ptolemy during the second century.

More important, he began his great treatise boldly by asserting that the sun lies at the center of the universe, but then he seems to have changed his mind. After the first few pages, Copernicus complicated what was otherwise a simple idea with unnecessary obfuscation. By the end of the book, he had placed the sun slightly off-center. Such prevarication makes the entire work almost unreadable and occasionally contradictory. At 212 sheets in small folio, the heart of *Revolutions* may be found in just the first twenty pages.

Because of the nature of the book, *Revolutions* did not make the immediate scientific impact it should have. Indeed, it went unnoticed by the Church for over seventy years after its first publication, only finding its way onto the *Index Librorum Prohibitorum* in 1616.[5]

Even so, Copernicus had been absolutely right to conceal his intentions and ideologies until he was beyond reach. In his treatise he had rejected wholesale the words of Aristotle on the key subject of astronomy, words describing unbending dogma that had for so long portrayed a false image of reality. For too long the egos of men had been soothed by what they had wanted to believe, the agony of insignificance muted by the geocentric model taught since ancient times and describing the planets and other celestial bodies revolving around the earth. "In the midst of all dwells the sun," Copernicus declared proudly in those clear and precise opening pages of his masterpiece. "Sitting on the royal throne, he rules the family of planets which turn around him. . . . We thus find in this arrangement an admirable harmony of the world."

Few words could have been more inflammatory, and gradually they reached their audience. Word-of-mouth played its crucial role, and slowly, a generation after the death of its author, *Revolutions* became the most famous and controversial book ever written.

---

5. And there it was to have good company. *Revolutions* was removed from the list in 1835, but the 1948 list (the last to be published) still included the entire works of Boyle, Hume, Hobbes, Voltaire, Zola, and, of course, Bruno. Contemporaries of Bruno's also found themselves on the list: Campanella's *City of the Sun* and Telesio's *De natura rerum iuxta propria principia* were both included from their date of publication. These were accompanied by *The History of the Decline and Fall of the Roman Empire, Madame Bovary*, works by Locke, Kant, Descartes, Fludd, Mill, and Bergson, and many of the most important literary treasures of modern civilization.

Long after the educated of Europe had devoured its contents and discovered its charms, *Revolutions* was burned in public by frenzied clerics. But in spite of the best efforts of the Church, books such as this could not go the way of flesh. *Revolutions* had already acted as an inspiration to those prepared to open their minds, those able and willing to accept a vision that opposed the traditional and comforting falsehoods the Holy Roman Church and Aristotle could offer. Copernicus's heretical heliocentric system became the foundation for an entirely new approach to natural philosophy, and it flung wide the intellectual floodgates. *Revolutions* showed clearly and irrefutably that Aristotle had been entirely wrong about the movement of the heavens. But, more important, it suggested that if Aristotle could be wrong about *that*, what of the other givens? What of the rest of Greek dogma so keenly adopted for their own ends by the theologians and popes? Perhaps these too were no less fanciful, no less misguided. The words of Copernicus were as shocking to men like Bruno as they were to the cardinals and the pope, but they produced opposite effects within each camp.

Bruno probably first learned of Copernicus when he was still a novice at the Monastery of St. Domenico. Naples had only come under the yoke of the Inquisition in 1547, so it is possible that the well-stocked library of the monastery still contained some unconventional books. Evidence to support Bruno's youthful introduction to Copernican heresy comes from a recently discovered mid-sixteenth-century edition of *Revolutions* found in the Biblioteca Casanatense in Rome. On the flyleaf of the book is the inscription "Brunus," written in a very ornate, rather juvenile style that suggests it could have been produced by a student. It is by no means certain that Bruno owned this book, but, knowing how from an early age he was thinking in heterodox terms and pushing his intellect beyond accepted wisdom, it is not difficult to visualize him blatantly adding his name to a book he probably even then understood to contain heretical ideas.[6]

But for Giordano Bruno, the shock of Copernicanism was not to be feared. Quite the opposite. Even as a young man he embraced *On the Revolutions of the Heavenly Spheres* as though it were a new Bible; indeed, to him it carried equal power and offered perhaps greater genuine insight. As stated at the start of this chapter, Giordano Bruno was no ordinary philosopher. He was well versed in the tradition of natural philosophy, but he was also cast from a very different mold than even those academics and learned clerics who dared to contemplate a universe not governed by Aristotelian principles. Bruno loathed those he perceived as dull-witted slaves to Aristotle; he abhorred the way advance was stultified by ancient misconceptions. Examples of how much he hatred mindless acceptance of traditional teaching proliferate in his books, but his most scathing attacks are to be found in *The Ash Wednesday Supper*, in which one of his lead characters refers to orthodox thinkers and followers of Aristotle as "the mob."[7]

But crucially, Bruno was an initiate of the occult tradition, and this alternate path running parallel with the progress of natural philosophy was one upon which Bruno traveled farthest. By the

6. See E. McMullin, "Bruno and Copernicus," *Isis* 78 (1987), pp. 55–74.
7. Giordano Bruno, *The Ash Wednesday Supper*, Dialogue I.

time he came to write his greatest works (in London and Paris and in Germany during the 1580s), when his talent was in full flower, he had already spent the greater part of his life studying the occult and the doctrine of pre-Christian religions. He had also readily absorbed traditional natural philosophy along with the latest ideas circulating among the intelligentsia of Renaissance Europe. Bruno acted as a vessel into which could flow the raw ideologies, the ingredients of human intellectual and intuitive endeavor, creating in him a gestalt, a union of the occult and protoscience. Others had provided fertile soil for such a blend, but none could add the special spice Bruno offered, none were nearly so brave, nor so determined.

The Hermetic tradition, the path of the occult, predates the route of natural philosophy by many millennia. To us, as to the people of the Renaissance, Greek knowledge is ancient knowledge, but the font of learning offered by the mystical, the intuitive, is far older still.

Some claim the occult tradition so treasured by many Renaissance figures can be traced to ancient Egypt; others place the source farther back in the fabled lost civilizations of Atlantis and Mu. According to legend, this secret knowledge was preserved by a chain of acolytes. From Hermes, the canon was supposedly passed on to the ancient Chaldeans (who are said to have founded the art of astrology). They donated their knowledge to another mythical figure, Orpheus, whose *Orphic Hymns* encapsulated much Egyptian learning. From Orpheus, Zoroaster became an initiate, followed by Pythagoras, Plato, and Plotinus. During the Renaissance the knowledge was adapted by Cornelius Agrippa, Paracelsus (Theophrastus Philipus Aureolus Bombastus von Hohenheim), Giovanni Pico della Mirandola, Masilio Ficino, and many others.

Although this may be largely speculation and legend, there is some evidence to show that a few elements of primitive magic and occult teachings were preserved from the Egyptian civilization, a period some two thousand years before Christ, but much of this arrived in Renaissance Europe in extremely distorted form. As late as the second century after Christ, obscure sects still worshiped in a few surviving Egyptian temples. Sun worship, a belief in the ability of magi to imbue life into inanimate objects by incantation, the empowering nature of symbols and ritual, and a devotion to astrology were core beliefs. A few rare texts from this time were copied, recopied, altered, and updated and eventually found their way to Alexandria, where they, along with the writings of Plato, Aristotle, and other Greeks, Alexandrians, and Romans filtered piecemeal into European culture.

For the intellectuals of the Renaissance, their source materials came as a result of a massive effort to rediscover the lost secrets of the ancients. This was certainly the most significant process in the flowering of the Renaissance itself. Today we live in an age when we habitually look forward rather than back to the past. Ours is a time during which we assume automatically the future will be more progressive, more enlightened, than the past, that we will know more and understand more tomorrow and still more the day after tomorrow. In our age, the past receives only lip service. But the Renaissance, as glorious and important as it undoubtedly proved to be, was a period during which thinkers viewed the past and the future in a way diametrically opposed to that of modern intellectuals. People of the Renaissance looked back upon past ages and saw a more sophisticated culture; theirs was a conviction that the ancients had access to a pool of knowledge and a unity of knowledge far superior to their own.

In some ways they were right; much *had* been lost and still more forgotten between the time of the Alexandrian philosophers and the reemergence of learning in the fourteenth century. But the idea of an ancient "grand understanding" was actually a fiction; the ancients had their own secrets but no truly overarching unity of knowledge, and they possessed no Ultimate Truth.

Yet, the Renaissance was also an expression of yearning for a new golden age modeled upon the wisdom of the ancients. As we have seen, emissaries were sent across the known world to find, buy, and, if necessary, steal any manuscripts or documents in the original Latin and Greek (for no one was then aware of the existence of tombs containing original Egyptian hieroglyphics). When these treasures were brought to Italy and translated, a vista of ancient learning, from Cicero to Plato, Homer to Hero, Aristotle to Archimedes, was opened up, and it acted as the seed for Renaissance neoclassicism.

As mentioned in chapter II, one of the most significant patrons for this expensive but highly rewarding search was the Medici family. Most conscientious was Cosimo de' Medici, who was born in Florence in 1389 and became one of the richest and most powerful men in Europe. Being a true model for the era in which he lived, Cosimo showed as much interest in Horace as he did in Hippocrates and had a lively fascination for the occult. In 1460, an anonymous monk came to him with a collection of Greek texts which, he claimed, were the original source material for all occult knowledge written by the ultimate authority, the man considered to be the font of all knowledge, Hermes Trismegistus. Cosimo was so captivated by this story he not only paid an exorbitant sum for the material but called upon his most trusted translator, Marsilio Ficino, to stop work on his almost completed translation of Plato to concentrate instead on this new collection. The result, completed a few months before Cosimo's death in 1464, was the *Corpus hermeticum*, a collection of fourteen volumes that energized the mystics, alchemists, and cabalists of the era more than any other occult text printed during the Renaissance.

But to a degree at least, Cosimo had been duped. The texts he had bought were not originals but dated from around the second century after Christ (the last period during which the ancient Egyptian religion was practiced openly) and were probably based on copies of copies of copies of a more ancient and purer text by then long lost.[8] But this mattered little; for the interested philosopher of the time, the *Corpus hermeticum* was an essential item, and it remained a cornerstone for the work of alchemists and mystics for at least two centuries after Cosimo's death. Indeed, no less a figure than Sir Isaac Newton possessed a copy, which he annotated with dense scribblings and used as a foundation for his own work as an alchemist.

Throughout the period during which ancient natural philosophy

---

8. This was revealed by the historian Isaac Casaubon in 1614.

was lost, then rediscovered by European theologians, the Hermetic tradition had also survived, kept alive and vibrant by generations of occultists who each added to the canon and watched it grow. Astrology, divination, symbol logic, alchemy, and ritualistic practices (including the black arts, demonology, and devil worship) thrived during the early Renaissance. Any individual could find what he wanted within the Hermetic tradition and could come away with his own treasure, his own magical directive.

It is clear from Bruno's writings that he was convinced by very little of the occult canon. To Bruno, as to many great thinkers after him, the occult was primarily a useful tool, a key that would open doors into arenas of thought and hidden depths of the human psyche. Along the occult path he found tracks, roughly hewn, that led to revelation and inspiration. Alchemy held no interest for Bruno; he was never motivated by experiment and was not drawn by the search for the philosophers' stone, the dream of limitless wealth. Neither did he practice ritualistic magic or necromancy; indeed, he often mocked practicing astrologers and many of the irrational precepts of witchcraft.[9]

Bruno was fully cognizant of the power of magic ritual and the occult tradition, but he knew much of it was superstition, wild fantasy, and wishful thinking.[10] He knew ritualistic magic pro-

---

9. Astrology has been perceived by many intellectuals as unworthy of serious consideration. Leonardo despised the court astrologer, Ambrogio Varese da Rosate, with whom he was obliged to work when under the patronage of the Duke of Milan, Ludovico Sforza, and Giovanni Pico della Mirandola wrote scathing attacks on the art in his *De astrologia*.

10. In one of his most important books, *Sigillus sigillorum* (*Seal of Seals*), Bruno writes with astonishing vision that the alchemists will not succeed in their inter-

duced results, but reasoned this was entirely due to the hypnotic power of the ritual itself. Symbols and incantations, he knew, could influence the mind powerfully, and the results depended upon the motivations of the participants. If one's intention was to corrupt or to destabilize, then the result might be defined as "black magic," whereas "white magicians" entered into the ritualistic process to produce a positive, or at least neutral, result. Either way, Bruno knew that the power of ritual stemmed from the mental and emotional characteristics of those involved and had nothing to do with external forces such as spirits or devils. The only force at work was the power of the human mind itself.

Bruno had a natural empathy for the pre-Christian theology of the ancient Egyptians and considered this closer to the source of Truth. For Bruno, ancient teachings possessed a purity and simplicity unsullied by a corrupt organization, whereas he considered the orthodox Church and its administration a destructive force.

Today, our perception of magic and the occult is quite different from that of people of the Renaissance. If we think about these things at all, we tend to visualize the occult as something dark and frightening, a plot element from a B movie, or perhaps we dismiss it as Disneyesque. But Bruno, who epitomized the approach of most intellectuals of the Renaissance, considered the

---

minable search for the philosophers' stone, but on their journey will stumble upon much that will be helpful to the natural philosopher. This proved to be quite true, because the alchemists achieved nothing of lasting theoretical value but were responsible for the invention of many valued laboratory techniques and the earliest designs of equipment still used today.

occult to be a pattern of ideas, a network of concepts that could be tapped into in order to gain a greater understanding of the universe. The Renaissance embodied the concept of fusing seemingly disparate disciplines, and the intelligentsia of the sixteenth century thought the same way about the occult. Many philosophers delighted in amalgamating ideas from the Hermetic tradition with natural philosophy, art, poetry, the study of language, rhetoric, medicine, music, even architecture and engineering in an attempt to produce a dynamic that could lead to great revelation. Indeed, what lies at the heart of Bruno's achievement is his belief that he could improve the world enormously by successfully fusing natural philosophy with the occult tradition, ancient religions, and Christianity.

Bruno began by developing a nonmathematical treatment of Copernicanism. This was both a way for him to understand the concepts and a method by which he could express the heliocentric model of Copernicus to students and laypeople who attended his lectures and read his books. But Bruno did not stop with such a shallow interpretation of Copernicus; he took it into areas none would have imagined.

And here a second obsession of Bruno's played a major role. From ancient religions and from his own reading and reasoning, he had reached an extreme form of Pantheism. For Bruno, the work of Copernicus could be used simply as a starting point, almost as a metaphor. To him, *Revolutions* was a foundation upon which he could build a doctrine of *universality*. Bruno believed in an infinite universe, a universe far greater than the cramped, rather ridiculous, parochial little place imagined by the Church fathers and theologians. He considered Copernicus's heliocentrism to be simplistic. Bruno's was a far more modern vision, one in which the sun was viewed as nothing more than one of many stars in an infinite firmament. In this philosophy, the people of the earth, the entire human race, should be considered as just another group of living things in a universe in which all was interconnected, each element interdependent and interrelated.

Bruno's vision was at once rooted in the sixteenth century and centuries ahead of his time. On the one hand, he saw a universe that bore no relationship to the orthodox model, but on the other, he cherished a close affinity with the ancient world and its ideologies. And of course, his convictions were outrageously heretical. Copernicus, still little noticed by the Church philosophers during the late sixteenth century, had offered a model that would soon be perceived by many of the faithful as the thin end of the wedge, anti-Aristotelian and dangerous; but Bruno's description trampled underfoot everything that was sacred.

Bruno's heresy was multifaceted. First, the notion of an infinite universe was anti-Aristotelian, but beyond this, even if it was a true description of the universe, it was such an esoteric, nebulous idea that the laity could never be made to understand it. The Church cherished simplicity in religious doctrine; the notion of a universe in which the sun and the earth were so devastatingly insignificant was simply unbearable. But still more extreme was Bruno's belief in the existence of intelligent life other than the human form on our own world. In his *De l'infinito universo et mondi* (*The Infinite Universe and Its Worlds*) of 1584, Bruno had written: "There are countless suns and an infinity of planets which circle round their suns as our seven planets circle round ours." This was perhaps the most dangerous notion of all, for, by implication, it denied one of the central precepts of orthodox Christianity, that Christ had died to cleanse this world and lead humanity to heaven. If other worlds existed with intelligent beings living there, did they have their own visitations? Did they nail their own Christs to a cross? The idea was quite unthinkable.

But Bruno did not stop even there. Inspired by Democritus and influenced by the mystical teachings of ancient Indian and Egyptian religions, he developed further his doctrine of universality. To him, the essence of a bee was indistinguishable from that of a human, the minerals of a rock were as significant as a pope. To Bruno, all things were recycled, all things interdependent. For this most extraordinary of thinkers, God existed in a ray of sunshine and in the soldier's sword, the whore's breath and the saint's healing robe. "This entire globe, this star, not being subject to death and dissolution and annihilation being impossible anywhere in Nature, from time to time renews itself by changing and altering all its parts. There is no absolute up or down, as Aristotle taught; no absolute position in space; but the position of a body is relative to that of other bodies. Everywhere there is incessant relative change in position throughout the universe, and the observer is always at the center of things."[11]

For Bruno, Copernicus, Horus of Egypt, Shiva, and the sun could coalesce, conjoin, and offer up miracles. And for him, none

---

11. Giordano Bruno, *De la causa, principio et uno* (*On Cause, Principle and the One*) (London, 1584).

of this diminished humankind; on the contrary, such an idea energized and invigorated, expanded and enlarged our importance in the universal scheme. The nineteenth-century German philosopher Ernst Cassirer said of Bruno's approach, "This doctrine was the first and decisive step towards man's self liberation. Man no longer lives in the world of a prisoner enclosed within the narrow walls of a finite, physical universe. The infinite universe sets no limits to human reason; on the contrary, it is the great incentive of human reason. The human intellect becomes aware of its own infinity through measuring its powers by the infinite universe."[12] We are part of a greater whole, Bruno believed; we are in direct communication with the divine, we are all part of the infinite. But to his enemies, infinity simply diminished, universality demeaned; and more than anything, it was this clash of ideologies that rested at the heart of their mutual hatred.

Yet, in spite of such adventurousness, Bruno's philosophy could be seen as little more than a loose collection of ideas, diaphanous, without anchor. But, to save it, there was one other element of Bruno's thinking that focused his view of the universe. To a love of God, an extreme Pantheism, a belief in the purity of original faith, and a model of universal Copernicanism, he added what would soon become a dying art, a branch of the Hermetic tradition no one today would even consider mystical at all, the "art of memory."

Bruno wrote five important books on memory, and although

---

12. Ernst Cassirer, *Essay on Man: Introduction to the Philosophy of Human Culture* (Berlin, 1944).

these are revelatory and contributed much to the discipline, they are but five of perhaps five thousand texts on the subject that were already in existence during the Renaissance.[13] During the entire sweep of human history up to the invention of the printing press, a prodigious memory was highly prized. Today we take for granted the ability to obtain information in whatever form on almost any subject. We have no need to recall the contents of our favorite novel, because it is always available for us to reread. We need not retain the memory of a symphony or the lines of a painting, because they are recorded and have been copied and copied again. If we are to make a speech, we can use an autocue; if we teach or preach, we rely upon a range of resources. But for the intellectual of the preprinting age, texts were scarce, hand-copied and extraordinarily expensive; little information was recorded and what little there was was often difficult to track down.

The art of memory (or mnemonics) is a subject that has been carefully documented since ancient times, and the Greeks, Romans, and Alexandrians expended considerable effort in developing ways to improve memory. By Bruno's time these techniques had reached a peak of sophistication but were already becoming anachronisms thanks to the proliferation of the printed word. Yet

---

13. Bruno's books on the art of memory are *De umbris idearum* (*The Shadow of Ideas*, 1582), *Cantus Circaeus ad eam memoriae praxim ordinatus quam ipse ludiciarum appellat* (*The Chant of Circe*, 1582), *Ars reminiscendi et in phantastico campo exarandi* (*The Art of Recollection*, 1583), *Lampas triginta statarum* (*The Lamp of Thirty Statues*, 1587), and *De imaginum, signorum et idearum compositione, ad omnia, inventionum, dispositonum et memoriae genera* (*On the Composition of Images, Signs and Ideas*, 1591).

for him, they still possessed a power that would provide another thread in his elaborate philosophical tapestry.

Bruno had a rich heritage upon which to draw. The first known book on the art of memory was *Ad herennium*, dating from around 80 B.C. and attributed to an anonymous Roman teacher. This was one of the first books translated into Italian, and copies found their way into the libraries of all the great thinkers of the age. The basic precepts of the art had remained unchanged through centuries of use. Aquinas and Magnus had been enthusiastic students of mnemonics and had written widely on the subject. The alchemists and mystics who followed the Hermetic path through the ages also utilized memory techniques to recall complex rituals and the details of convoluted experiments. Often, to protect their secrets, they had subjected their findings to memory rather than recording them in written form.

The essence of the art is the ability to enhance memory by a process of mechanical mental exercises. If a complex array of information is to be remembered it must first be separated into sections relevant to different subjects. These must then be placed into some sort of order, perhaps hierarchical, alphabetical, or chronological. Then each manageable piece of information is attached to an easily recalled material item. This could be a place, an object, or a person. The best example is a method for memorizing a diverse and lengthy list of names, numbers, or any other collection of information. First, the list is broken down into sections, then the more manageable chunks are assigned to a room in a house. Within each room the several pieces of information related to it are assigned to different objects in that room. If this technique is adhered to closely, vast amounts of data may be recalled by mentally wandering through the house and "picking up" objects to which information has been assigned.

Certainly a useful party trick. But to Bruno, his contemporaries, and his forebears, this technique and other similar methods devised by the ancients represented far more than a game. For Bruno, the art of memory was a prized method of remembering and recalling all he had learned, and if blended with the occultist's fascination for symbols, it could provide a structure for his carefully designed Christian-Hermetic system. Bruno believed that an enhanced memory could boost the power of the individual psyche so that the human mind, and with it the spirit, could tap into the greater imprint of the universe.

To understand this, we must piece together Bruno's philosophy stage by stage. First came the concept of universality and infinity. Bruno insisted the individual and the race were elemental parts of a unit, that there is a universe in us and we are part of the universe. Second were the pure forms of ancient religion combined with the beauty of Christ's original teachings along with those of other great prophets and ancient magi. Next came the new visions provided by the embryonic "science" of the time. Natural philosophy had created a doctrine to transcend and supersede the false notions of Aristotle, reveal the corruption of the Church, and clear the obfuscation generated by the Council of Nicaea. Last, these combined notions could be understood and represented by occult symbols and rituals (not unlike the way

Christianity was also portrayed through symbols and rituals) but made accessible with a mind empowered by a boosted memory.

Bruno looked out upon a world in which the vast majority of people understood little of the things they worshiped. For most people of the age, driven by fear, God was an all-powerful Creator and ultimate authority. But in equal measure, the common folk also feared Nature, the imagined spirit world, and witchcraft. Bruno believed he could raise the minds and the spirits of men above this tawdry existence, emancipate, enrich, and empower. Each individual, he believed, each element of the great universe, each part of the One, could understand and draw upon the whole to make an infinitely better world.

Bruno produced some thirty books during a writing career spanning two decades.[14] In these, his seemingly complex (yet, at its core, wonderfully simple) doctrine grew and developed. Some of these works, such as his last published work, *De imaginum, signorum et idearum compositione* (*On the Composition of Images, Signs and Ideas*), concentrated on the art of memory. Others, most important *La cena de le ceneri* (*The Ash Wednesday Supper*) and *De la causa, principio et uno* (*On Cause, Principle and the One*), both from 1584, are attacks on Aristotle and develop Bruno's unique universal Copernicanism. Another of his most famous works, still in print in English, is *Spaccio de la bestia trionfante* (*The Expulsion of the Triumphant Beast*), the

---

14. Many of these have been lost, and some were never published. Bruno also wrote at least two plays. The best-known of these is *Il Candelaio* (*The Torch-Bearer*), a satirical comedy composed during his first sojourn in Paris around 1582. (See Appendix III.)

last of a quartet of masterpieces all written and published in London in 1584.[15] In this, perhaps his most accomplished literary work, he uses the allegory of an internal struggle among the pagan gods of the ancient world to rip into the authority of the Church, satirizing, mocking, and exposing the inconsistencies and weaknesses of what he saw as a manmade religion fabricated by the Council of Nicaea. In his final work, *De vinculis in genere* (*On Links in General*), left incomplete and unpublished after his arrest in Venice, Bruno came close to unifying the disparate elements of his philosophy into a cogent whole. This was a book that might well have become his most complete testament, the book he was completing when he returned to Italy and was trying to supervise through the press when he was arrested in Venice. *De vinculis in genere* also formed the basis of the document Bruno wished to present to the pope explaining his doctrine.

With his most accomplished works published in 1584 and within the surviving fragments of *De vinculis in genere*, Bruno had produced a collection of tracts that went a long way toward creating a grand synthesis, an all-embracing new philosophy representing an original mental paradigm. He had, he believed, done nothing less than woven the fabric for a new religion. But what did he hope to achieve with his work? What had been his goal through two decades of effort, and what remained of his mission as he left Frankfurt for Italy?

To answer this we need to recall the political and religious

---

15. The other book in this quartet is *De l'infinito universo et mondi* (*On the Infinite Universe and Its Worlds*), another great work of nonmathematical cosmology.

struggles that dominated Europe during the sixteenth century. As we have seen, Renaissance Europe was a civilization at a crossroads, about to step into a future of global trade, a massive expansion in the ways people communicated, traveled, and recorded information, but it remained grounded by ideological conflict. As Bruno traveled Europe, the Counter Reformation was in full swing, the witch-hunts had become the favorite sport of the Inquisitors, and Europe was embroiled in a succession of bloody conflicts initiated by doctrinal clashes and endemic intolerance.

The true powder keg of conflict was produced by the ideological clash between Catholics and Protestants, and Bruno, a disillusioned Catholic, but unconvinced by Protestantism, held an unshakable personal conviction that he could straddle the divide between these factions. His method had nothing to do with diplomacy or debate and everything to do with wiping the slate clean and presenting a fresh page upon which a new doctrine could be inscribed. Bruno was convinced that liberal thinkers among both Protestant and Catholic could understand his vision, appreciate it, and eventually adopt it wholeheartedly.

Typically, his method for trying to achieve this goal was idiosyncratic to say the least. During the 1580s, he did not view himself as a Luther or a Calvin, but he knew he could communicate, knew he was a gifted and charismatic teacher. His best chance of making a significant mark, he believed, was to influence those far more powerful and better-connected than himself. Instead of pushing himself forward as some sort of messiah of the new age, he intended to use someone universally recognized as a world-class statesman. Bruno would educate him, inspire him with his revolutionary philosophy, and through this figure establish a new world order based upon a deep spirituality, a universality, a Christian Hermeticism.

With his first attempt he planned to use Henry III of France. The two men became close, and Bruno seems to have greatly influenced the king's thinking, but eventually political pressures in a country which in recent years had experienced the fullest extremes of internecine religious conflict were too much even for Henry's diplomatic skills and aggressive individualism. Still holding faith with Bruno's ideas, however, Henry encouraged Bruno to journey across the English Channel, where his philosophies would be more favorably received by the relatively liberal-minded English court. To facilitate his entrée into the highest echelons of English society, Bruno was put in direct contact with Henry's ambassador in London, Michel de Castelnau.

It can be no coincidence that Bruno composed his greatest work in London between 1583 and 1585. He was in full bloom, confident and clear-sighted. His synthesis of universal Copernicanism, Christianity, and the occult had matured, and he was able to express his ingenious doctrine using the vehicle of drama and dialogue (a technique Galileo and others would later copy). And in England he found his second chance to educate and convert a monarch, a figure powerful enough, given the necessary philosophical materials, to influence the minds of men and bring dramatic change.

To Bruno, Elizabeth was the universal, utopian monarch, the one who could unite and clarify, enlighten and advance. She also shared many of Henry's spiritual preoccupations. She surprised

European leaders by conferring upon Henry the Order of the Garter, and for a short period around the time of Bruno's visit to London relations between England and France were exceptionally cordial; there was even talk of the two countries forming an antipapal league. But Bruno's hope was misplaced. As fond of Henry as Elizabeth may have been, she had absolutely no intention of attempting to unite Catholics and Protestants through philosophy. She certainly wished for unity, but only by conventional means, the diplomatic letter and the blades of her soldiers. Elizabeth was a monarch who relied heavily upon a rostrum of advisers and guides; her more conservative ministers loathed her interest in the magus John Dee, but at least he was English. Bruno, who was perceived by many Englishmen as a loud, overexpressive, abrasive little man, would have grated on and antagonized them, and indeed, within two years of meeting Elizabeth, he returned to mainland Europe disillusioned, his confidence in tatters.

Bruno's aim was to bring together the liberals in each camp, and key to accomplishing this was to find a way in which Protestants and Catholics could agree over the meaning of the Eucharist, a concept that lay at the heart of both faiths. Of all the doctrinal incompatibilities between Rome and the Protestant religion, the *interpretation* of the Eucharist was the most profound. Protestants held the view that the earthly components of the Eucharist simply *represented* the flesh and the blood of the Lord, but this was not good enough for Catholics. Rome insisted that the communion meant quite literally partaking of divine matter; during the sacrament of Eucharist service the bread and the wine were transubstantiated into the flesh and blood of the Savior.

Bruno wanted to treat the Eucharist as a supreme example of how conflict could be negated. His interpretation of the process was one of union. The bread and the wine, just like the chalice and the cloth, the priestly robes, the stone of the church, and the saliva of the believers, were all one and the same. By drinking the wine and swallowing the bread, the faithful conjoined with the great "oneness of the universe." By creating this third way, Bruno imagined he could end the disagreement over the Eucharist. And if this was possible, then all doctrinal disagreements might be overcome with equal grace.

Bruno's *Ash Wednesday Supper* is probably his most widely read book and the most absorbing. It focuses upon a supper held in Westminster, not far from where Bruno was living at the time (the French ambassador's home near Fleet Street). The guests invited to the meal constitute a select group of London's intelligentsia, and over the meal they discuss their beliefs and debate the issues uppermost in Bruno's mind. Of course, the supper is allegorical, and the food and the wine are the materials of the Eucharist, then at the heart of Bruno's philosophical concerns. The story begins with a discussion about Copernicus and develops, through his interlocutors, into the theme of universal Copernicanism, which offers up the notion Bruno saw as a unifying force, the concept of the Oneness of Nature.

Bruno found new followers in England and nurtured already well established relationships. The most important was his friendship with the famous courtier, soldier, diplomat, and poet Philip Sidney, but even this relationship did not further his chances of finding a practical solution to the conflict between Catholic and

Protestant. Bruno's books, although influential and widely read by the educated elite, did not impress Elizabeth herself, nor anyone of great importance at court other than Sidney.

Also, to be fair to Bruno, the political kaleidoscope of European politics and religious allegiance had been shaken again while he was in England. During the summer of 1585, Henry's mother, Catherine de Médicis, a brilliant diplomat despite being in her sixty-seventh year and riddled with syphilis, had negotiated a temporary peace between French Protestants and Catholics that effectively kept foreign powers out of her son's kingdom. Although these actions provided only a temporary solution to the religious problems of Europe, fickle monarchs and ambitious politicians turned their attention elsewhere for a time. Consequently, by October 1585, Bruno was once more in Europe and attempting to find a new avenue for his convictions.

For five years, he continued to write, to lecture widely, and to develop many important new friendships during the travels that occupied these remaining years of freedom. And by 1590, or perhaps as late as the beginning of 1591, Bruno had reached the conclusion that if he was to have any serious hope of attaining his goal of uniting the splintered world of religion, there was only one man who could help him do it, the pope himself.

During the months before his decision to return to Italy, Bruno was living in Germany and Switzerland, far from Rome, far from danger. He could have remained in either of these places, patronized by wealthy cabalists and occultists; he could have found teaching positions and enjoyed some security. Yet, this would also have meant defeat, capitulation, stagnation. This he could not face. Instead, he turned away from convention once more by shunning the easy path. He began his final work, a grand summation of his entire canon, a document to encapsulate his whole doctrine and one that would, he believed, captivate and enthral the pope. This is why, in October 1591, he packed his trunks, collected together his papers, persuaded his amanuensis Herman Besler to accompany him, and set forth on the road from Frankfurt to teach the nobleman Mocenigo in the land of his forefathers, the land he had fled twelve years earlier.

· V ·

THE VENETIAN TRIAL

If, most illustrious gentleman, I worked a plow, pastured a flock, cultivated an orchard, and tailored a garment, no one would look at me, few would observe me, by very few would I be reprehended and I could easily be pleasing to everybody. But since I am a delineator of the field of nature, solicitous concerning the pasture of the soul, enamored of the cultivation of the mind, and a Daedalus as regards the habits of the intellect, behold one who, having cast his glance upon me, threatens me, one who, having observed me, assails me, another who, having attained me, bites me, and another who, having apprehended me, devours me. It is not one person, it is not a few, it is many, it is almost all.

—Giordano Bruno

THE TRIAL OF Giordano Bruno began on May 26, 1592, in the Patriarchal Palace, positioned opposite the prison on the Rio di Palazzo. Unlike the Roman Inquisition, the Venetian equivalent was at least accountable to the government. The Romans could get away with almost anything because all trials were held in secret; in Venice one of three assessors for the state called *savii all'eresia,* who were changed every year and who remained under the direction of the governor throughout a trial, reported each day all that happened in court. Three judges were present at each hearing (the patriarch and two others) and were known collectively as "the Three." Accompanying them was the assessor, who could halt the proceedings immediately if he believed the trial deviated from the letter of the law.

Hearings of the Venetian Inquisition were not merely show trials; the state was proud of its oligarchical system and placed great importance upon procedure and legal correctness. However, though they were liberal for the time, such trials ran according to legal processes we would barely recognize today. Bruno was allowed no advocate and had to answer his charges alone. He was given no time for preparation, no access to information, texts, precedents, or indeed any form of communication with the outside world. And, empowered by the Bulls of Innocent IV, *Cum negocium* and *Licet sicut acceptimus*, both delivered in 1250, the court at no time provided Bruno with the name of his accuser, only the claims against him. Furthermore, although it was a self-regulated body and the presence of the assessor was respected, the records of the hearing were never made public, all processes were conducted in private, and everyone involved was constrained by an oath of silence. Most alarming, Bruno's judges were skilled and practiced in the art of extracting information from the accused, experts in twisting words and leading both witnesses and victims into unwise admissions. These men were ecclesiastics who wished to portray the view that the earthly realm meant little, that the world to come was everything. They placed little importance upon the physical well-being of the accused and believed they could do almost anything in the name of God. Fired up by prejudice, ener-

gized by peer pressure, and with dogma and conviction as suste-
nance, they wielded immense, terrifying power. Although the
Venetian state had moved closer to egalitarianism than any other
Western society, we must never forget that powerful men of the
sixteenth century had, almost without exception, acquired their
power through cruelty, ambition, and ruthless energy; dealing
with such men demanded caution.

Bruno's trial was represented for the state by the current patriarch, Laurentio Priuli, a former Venetian ambassador to Paris. The
other two judges were the apostolic nuncio, Ludovico Taberna,
and the Father Inquisitor, the Very Reverend Father Giovanni
Gabrielle of Saluzzo. The panel was completed by Aloysio Fuscari, the assessor. During the days leading up to the hearing, the
three judges had read, in private conclave, two specially prepared
reports written for them by Bruno's accuser, Giovanni Mocenigo.

In the first, composed on May 24, the day after Bruno's arrest,
Mocenigo begins by describing his motivations for deceiving
Bruno. "I am compelled by my conscience and the order of my
Confessor," he writes, and then goes on to offer clear evidence of
the contrite nature of his actions against Bruno and how, all
along, he was serving his Inquisition masters. "Since you have
favored me with so much forbearance by pardoning my error in
delaying my tardy accusation, I pray you to excuse it before these
Illustrious Lords, since my intention was good; for I could not get
at the whole matter at once; nor did I know the vileness of the
man until I had kept him in my house some two months . . . and
then I desired to get the better of him and by my dealings with
him could be certain that he would not make off without my

knowledge. Thus I have always assured myself of being able to make him come under the censure of the Holy Office. This I have succeeded in doing."[1]

In this first statement it appears Mocenigo is trying to recover from some embarrassment or an error he had made during the process. It may have been that Mocenigo had convinced both himself and his masters that Bruno would be any easy catch. Bruno's initial refusal to stay in Mocenigo's palace must have been a galling setback and delayed the Inquisition's plans.

The apologies over, Mocenigo then offered what constituted his gathered evidence against Bruno, a confection of undoubtedly accurate statements along with half-truths, exaggerations, and what was almost certainly plain fiction.

"At various times when he has talked with me at home [he] said that Catholics were much to blame in holding that bread becomes flesh; that he was an enemy of the Mass; that no religion pleases him; that Christ was a wretch; that he might very well foretell his being hanged, since he did evil to seduce the people. [Bruno said] that there was no distinction of Persons of God, which would be an imperfection; that the world is eternal and that there are infinite worlds, and that God unceasingly makes infinities because he wills as much as he can. [Bruno claimed] that Christ worked miracles in appearance and was a magician; the same of the Apostles, and that he might be given the mind to do as much and more; that Christ showed he was unwilling to die, and put it off as long as he could; that there is no punishment of

---

1. Doc. i.

sins, and that souls, created by the operation of nature, pass from one animal to another, and that, even as brute beasts are born of corruption, so are men, who are born again after deluges."

This hodgepodge is fascinating because of the sheer breadth of the accusations. Clearly, some of Mocenigo's claims are rather hackneyed and strikingly similar to those found in the statements made against other known heretics. Indeed, it is hard to imagine anyone in the religious climate of the time admitting to someone they hardly knew their conviction that they were "an enemy of the Mass; that no religion pleases him; that Christ was a wretch; that he might very well foretell his being hanged, since he did evil to seduce the people."

However, other remarks fit neatly into Bruno's worldview. His claims for reincarnation and transmigration of souls would not have been alien to him, as these were ideas derived from many ancient religions with which he was quite familiar. The idea that men and other animals are, in essence, one and the same—"even as brute beasts are born of corruption, so are men"—is entirely consistent with Bruno's pantheism. And, of course, infinite worlds and the eternal nature of the physical realm are core Bruno beliefs. Furthermore, claims that Bruno condemned the concept of the Holy Trinity could be hardly surprising, as it lay at the foundation of Bruno's support for Arianism; the only surprise is that Bruno should confess to such extreme heresy.

Mocenigo's statement continued:

"He set forth a design to form a new sect, under the name of the New Philosophy; said the Virgin could not have brought forth a child, and that our Catholic faith is full of blasphemy against the

Majesty of God; that the disputes and revenues of friars should be stopped, because they befoul the earth; that they are asses and their doctrines asinine; that we have no proof that our faith is endorsed by God, and that to abstain from doing to others what we are unwilling they should do to us is enough for a good life; he is in favor of all other sins, and that it is a marvel God endures so many heresies of Catholics; he says he desires to apply himself to divination, and all the world would follow him; that St. Thomas (Aquinas) and all the doctors knew nothing, and that he could enlighten the first theologians in the world so that they would be unable to reply."[2]

Mocenigo ends with a reminder that the Inquisition had prepared a total of no fewer than 130 charges against Bruno, starting with his desertion of the Monastery of St. Domenico. He stated his belief that Bruno was possessed by the Devil and that others would bear witness to his claims, including the Venetian booksellers Ciotto (Giovanni Battista) and Andrea Morosini. Mocenigo then accompanied this statement with a collection of items stolen from Bruno, including three printed works by other philosophers and a manuscript believed to have been penned by Bruno himself.

Again, this part of Mocenigo's statement contains a similar blend of fact and fiction. It is highly unlikely Bruno would have expressed such feelings about Aquinas. Ironically we have here one of the faithful (Mocenigo) using an example of a favored figure from orthodox theology (Aquinas) to hold a claim of heresy

---

2. Doc. i.

against Bruno; but Aquinas had two faces: the one adopted by later churchmen as the epitome of Catholic convention; the other, unknown beyond the circle of European occultists, that of the mystic and alchemist.

Again Mocenigo goes too far and slides into cliché. When Bruno merely repeats the words of Christ, "to abstain from doing to others what we are unwilling they should do to us is enough for a good life," his betrayer adds, ". . . he is in favor of all other sins."

Yet, the most damaging accusation is Mocenigo's contention that Bruno wanted to debase the Church and create a new sect. In making this assumption Mocenigo had nothing to go on but hearsay. Rumors about Bruno's intentions had been circulating among underground figures since his return from England, and some may have assumed that the only move Bruno could make would be to follow the example of others and gather initiates to form a sect. Bruno had, however, surprised everyone by returning to Italy with just one servant.

Nevertheless, a central concern for the Inquisition was the fear that heretics might effectively challenge orthodox theology. They had plenty of reason to fear such a thing, Luther and Calvin were only the most famous and successful examples of the heterodox rebelling against the established Church. Hundreds of other sects had come and gone in recent centuries, and the hard attitude of the Church only encouraged revolution. More than any single quality, the Catholic Church cherished the notion of its own uniqueness; its, it believed, was the singular true path to enlightenment, and the pope, in direct communion with the One God, was the only guide to heaven. Leaders of the Holy Church had discarded the lives of tens of thousands of crusaders as though they were worthless garbage, and through the use of the Inquisition, they had exterminated tens of thousands of innocents, scything humanity without compunction in order to maintain the authority of the Vatican and its incredible hold over the faithful. Naturally, then, any deviation from orthodoxy was deemed intolerable. In the eyes of the pope, the Inquisition, the Dominicans, and the Franciscans, the offense of the heretic was always the same, the heinous crime of attempting to undermine the status quo. Every statement of the accusers offered a belief that the poor soul on trial was attempting to create disorder and to supplant the God-given power of Rome.

Yet, strikingly, in Bruno's case, Mocenigo's statement seems to have fallen short, because after submitting this missive, he was asked to furnish a second statement before the trial could begin. So, as Bruno languished in his cell not knowing what was to happen to him, completely isolated from the outside world and unaware of the deliberations surrounding his arrest, Mocenigo dredged his memory for more evidence and wrote:

"On the day when I held Bruno locked up, I asked him if he would fulfill his promises concerning what he proved unwilling to teach me in return for my many acts of kindness and gifts, so that I might not accuse him of so many wicked words to me against our Lord Jesus Christ and the Holy Catholic Church. He replied that he had no dread of the Inquisition, for he had offended no one in his way of living and could not recall having said anything wicked; and, even if he had done so, he had said it to me without any witness being present, and therefore he did not fear that I could injure him in that way, and even if I should be handed over to the Inquisition, they could only force him to resume his habit. 'So you were a monk,' said I. He replied, 'I took the first habit, and therefore, in any case, I could readily adjust matters.' I followed up with, 'And how can you adjust your affairs if you do not believe in the most Holy Trinity; if you say such wicked things of Our Lord Jesus Christ; if you hold our souls to be made of filth and everything in the world guided by Fate, as you have told me on several occasions? You must needs first adjust your opinions, and the rest will be easy; and if you wish, I will give you all the aid I can, that you may know that, although you have so broken your word and been so ungrateful for all my kindness, I still wish in every way to be your friend.' At this he only prayed me to set him free; if he had packed his things and told me he wished to leave, he did not mean it, but wished to bridle my impatience to be taught, wherein I perpetually tormented him, and, if I would set him at liberty, he would teach me all he knew; moreover, he would disclose the secret of all his works to me alone; also, that he meditated writing others, which should be beautiful and exceptional; he would be my slave with no further reward than what I have given; and, if I wanted all he had in my house, it should be mine, for in every way he owed everything to me: all he wanted was a little book of conjurations which I found among his writings"[3]

In some ways this is a more potent account than the first.

---

3. Doc. ii. The "book of conjurations" Mocenigo writes of was *The Seals of Hermes and Ptolemy*, known to have been in Bruno's possession at the time of his capture.

Mocenigo here seems to be running away with himself in a desperate effort to convince the Inquisition he has carried through the job assigned to him. At the beginning of this statement he becomes so wrapped up in his claims that he reaches an amazing tautology by telling Bruno he will not report him if the magus will finally submit to teaching him the occult arts.

In most ways, though, this second statement is little more than a reiteration of the first, for Mocenigo had clearly run out of ideas or accusations to pin on Bruno. The fact that Bruno had formerly been a monk was certainly no news at all, and the further hints that Bruno was planning to write more heretical texts and wanted only to keep a "little book of conjurations" is merely further spice for the judges. It also carries with it further suggestions that Mocenigo had tried desperately hard to ensnare Bruno and had acted with vigilance and determination; Mocenigo never missed an opportunity for self-aggrandizement. Yet, despite working hard to portray himself as a benevolent, faithful Christian who wanted to bring the heretic to enlightenment, Mocenigo's characterization of Bruno was ridiculously muddled. Bruno was certainly a heretic, but he was definitely not a man to beg for mercy because a nobleman had placed him under house arrest.

And yet, in spite of the inconsistencies and the sheer amateurishness of Mocenigo's writing and the actions described in his report, the Venetian judges were swayed by it enough to endorse the arrest and to place Giordano Bruno on trial before the Inquisition, believing such a move lawful and justifiable. Of course, they had wanted to do this all along, but they needed to support the decision with sufficient evidence. Mocenigo's report was shoddy, to say the least; however, to men who knew nothing of Bruno's character (and little if anything of his philosophies) but were keen to persecute a heretic, it was good enough. The trial was set to begin the following day, Tuesday, May 26, 1592.

The court was positioned in the heart of the complex of buildings around the Doges' Palace, the windows barred and the doors guarded at all times. The judges and the assessor, resplendent in their robes of office, sat in high-backed, cushioned chairs on a raised platform and formed a small arch with a bare wooden stool for the accused facing them. To one side, the witnesses stood facing the rest of the court. On the other side were two rows of chairs for government officials and senior public figures there by invitation and sworn to secrecy. The clerk to the court sat in a lower part of the room close to the witnesses so he could report everything he saw and heard.

First to be called to the chair was one of Bruno's inner circle in Venice, Giovanni Battista, often known as Ciotto. Ciotto was a man long used to the system employed by the Inquisition. As a seller of arcane literature, some of which undoubtedly crossed the invisible line between orthodoxy and heresy, he would have been as well equipped as anyone could be to face the sort of questions posed by Laurentio Priuli, Ludovico Taberna, and the Father Inquisitor, Giovanni Gabrielle.

Father Gabrielle began by asking Ciotto to describe how he came to know of Mocenigo and his links with Giordano Bruno. Ciotto replied in a matter-of-fact manner. "I was about to start for the Frankfurt Fair last Easter when Signor G. Mocenigo found me and asked me if I were going thither. He said: 'I have him [Giordano Bruno] here at my expense. He has promised to teach me many things and has had a quantity of clothes and money from me on this account. I can bring him to no conclusion. I doubt whether he is quite trustworthy. So, since you are going to Frankfurt, keep this in mind, and do me the service to find out if anyone has faith in him and if he will carry out his promises.' By reason of this, when I was in Frankfurt I spoke with several scholars who had attended his lectures when he was in the city and were acquainted with his method and discourse. What they told me amounted to this, that Giordano made strong professions of memory and other similar secrets, but success with anyone was never seen, and his pupils in this matter and others similar were far from satisfied. They said more. They did not know how he could remain in Venice, for he is regarded as a man without religion. This is all I gathered, and I told it to Ser Giovanni when I returned from the fair, whereto he replied: 'I also had my doubts of this; but I wish to find out what I can draw from him of the instructions he has promised me, not to lose altogether what I have given him, and then I shall hand him over to the Censure of the Holy Office.' "[4]

This is the statement of a cautious man placed in a dangerous situation. The Venetian authorities certainly did not turn an entirely blind eye to the selling of occult literature, but neither were they keen to stifle any form of trade, the lifeblood of the city, so a delicate mutual respect enabled the tradesmen to prosper and the ecclesiastics to remain content. However, before the Inquisi-

---

4. Doc. v.

tion, men like Ciotto had to tread very carefully, even in Venice. On the one hand, if their account lent too much sympathy for the prosecution, then they would be seen within the community of occultists as untrustworthy and their businesses would suffer. On the other, if they offered too much support for the accused, they could be suspected themselves and face similar persecution over their own often questionable affairs.

Consequently, Ciotto's statement says very little. He abrogates any remarks that might be construed as suspicious by placing comments in the mouths of others, and it is clear that what he told Mocenigo was meant to dissuade the man from persisting with Bruno. We must remember that Ciotto was an associate of Bruno's; everything in this statement points to an attempt to both underplay Bruno's art and to distance himself from it without slandering Mocenigo or anyone else.

Next to offer evidence was another bookseller of Bruno's acquaintance, Jacobus Britanus, a middle-aged man from Antwerp who had lived in Venice for some years and was known to Italians as Giacomo Bertano. The bookseller was read a section of Mocenigo's first statement, in which his name had been used to support Mocenigo's accusations against Bruno. Father Gabrielle's voice cut through the silence of the courtroom as he repeated Mocenigo's words:

"'Britanus in particular spoke of him to me, declaring him to be an enemy of Christianity and our faith, and that he had heard him utter great heresy.' What say you to this?"[5]

---

5. Doc. i.

Britanus, another friend of Bruno's, another who had shared with him Hermetic secrets in the darkened rooms of mutual acquaintances, stared resolutely at the Father Inquisitor. "I utterly refute that statement," he said crisply. "He was chiefly occupied in writing and in the vain and chimerical imagining of novelties," he added.

The clerk to the court then reported that the patriarch, Laurentio Priuli, rose and adjoined the court until the following Friday, May 29.

On the morning of the twenty-ninth, Britanus was questioned once more and claimed he knew nothing of Bruno's character, that they had hardly discussed religion or spiritual matters and that he was only vaguely acquainted with Bruno. The court adjourned for lunch, and in the afternoon, Bruno was, for the first time, subjected to cross-examination. As Bruno took his seat, the clerk to the court recorded his impressions of the prisoner. "Giordano Bruno is," he wrote, ". . . of ordinary height, with a chestnut-colored beard and looking about his age of forty."[6]

The atmosphere was tense and Bruno was very nervous. Just as Priuli ordered the accused to tell the truth, Bruno suddenly burst out: "I *shall* tell the truth. Often I have been threatened with the Holy Office and I deemed it a joke; so I am quite ready to furnish an account of myself."[7] As he spoke, his voice trembled and he waved his hands before him, gesticulating earnestly. For six days Bruno had been left alone in his tiny cell to contemplate his fate,

6. Doc. iii.
7. Doc. vii.

and now perhaps for the first time he had come to realize the seriousness of the situation. Perhaps for the first time he caught the distant crackle of flames, the faint whiff of his own burning flesh.

The judges appraised the man before them. They had been furnished with copies of some of his works, which they had read with growing disdain, and they had been provided with a report on Bruno's life, his travels, his ideas, and his philosophy. As the court fell silent, and Bruno, a small, disheveled figure sat, Gabrielle leaned forward in his chair and began the questioning. The exchange of question and answer continued without a break long into the evening of May 29, and from this and subsequent days of interrogation a picture of Bruno began to emerge, his life story and the beliefs and convictions to which he was then willing to admit. The records of these represent the only surviving account of the chronology of Bruno's life. What follows is an amalgamation of his statements that help to construct an image of Bruno, the heretic.

※

He was born Felipe Bruno in the tiny town of Nola at the foot of Mount Vesuvius close to Naples; ashes were in his blood. The monastery he had been sent to seemed to the boy to be an enchanted place where his natural inclination for learning could be best encouraged. Only as he grew older and learned more, only as he began to conceive a broader canvas, could he see fissures in what he was taught, anomalies, inconsistencies, and lies.

"One day," he told the court, "during a discussion with Montalcino, one of our order, in the company of other fathers, he

[Montalcino] said that heretics were ignorant folk and used no scholastic terms; whereto I replied that indeed they did not set forth their conclusions in the scholastic manner; but they came to the point, as did the fathers of the Church. Then I showed the view of Arius to be less dangerous than it was commonly taken to be; for it was generally understood that Arius meant to teach that the Word was the first creation of the Father; and I explained that Arius said the Word was neither Creator nor Created, but intermediary between the Creator and the creature, just as the spoken word is an intermediary between the speaker and the meaning he sets forth; and that, for this reason, it is called the First-born before all creatures, through which, and out of which all things are; not to which, but through which all things return to their final end, which is the Father."[8]

In 1576, Bruno fled the monastery after he had been threatened with an appearance before the local Inquisitor where he would have faced charges of harboring heretical views and reading forbidden texts. He changed his name and discarded his cowl. For short periods he found sanctuary in local monasteries, but always his reputation caught up with him and he was forced to move on in the still of night, traveling through the darkened countryside to the next temporary haven, ever wary, ever fearful.

Placing faith in a place in which he hoped he would become anonymous, he headed for Rome. He wished to be allowed to settle there, to teach, to write in peace, but he was to stay only a few weeks before moving on once more, the authorities ever only

8. Doc. xi.

one step behind him. "I learned," he admitted, "that after leaving Naples, certain works of St. Chrysostom and St. Jerome containing the forbidden annotations of Erasmus, which I had secretly used and thrown into the privy when I came away to prevent their being found, were discovered."[9] Soon after this, he learned that he had been excommunicated *in absentia.*

Now nowhere in Italy was safe for him. In his statement to the Inquisition, Mocenigo had reported that Bruno had "told me that the Inquisition sought a quarrel with him in Rome on 130 points, and that he made off while they were being presented because he was credited with throwing the informer, or the man whom he believed to be such, into the Tiber."[10]

Our knowledge of this episode is further confused by a statement found in the diary of a librarian named Guillaume Cotin whom Bruno met during the mid-1580s. The diary was discovered during the nineteenth century in the Bibliothèque Nationale and is believed to be genuine. In it, Cotin remarks: "7th December. [1585]. Jordanus came again. . . . He has been an exile from Italy eight years, as much by reason of a murder committed by his brother [meaning a fellow priest], whereby he incurred hatred and peril of life, as to escape the calumnies of Inquisitors, who are ignorant men, and, not understanding his philosophy, declare him to be a heretic."[11]

Strikingly, at the Venetian trial (and later in Rome) the

---

9. Doc. xiii.
10. Doc. i.
11. M.S. Fr 20309, fol. 345, V.sqq. Bibliothèque Nationale.

Inquisitors appeared to have no interest in this incident and ignored this attempt of Mocenigo's to sensationalize further his claims against the Nolan. Clearly Bruno had become involved with some disreputable characters in Rome. He was, we must always remember, a fugitive. He was living in the very bosom of the enemy, walking the same roads, sharing the very air the Inquisitors breathed. By necessity he would have been forced to live furtively, associating with criminals and other heretics, away from unwanted gaze. But the Inquisitors now seemed to have little interest in the events in Rome; either they had been satisfied of his innocence or else they had decided to ignore the issue because they did not want the question of a possible murder, however distant, to overshadow the claims of heresy.[12]

Whatever the circumstances of Bruno's involvement in this murder, immediately after the incident, he was prompted to act more resolutely than he had since leaving his order. He immediately left the capital, temporarily reverted to his Christian name of Felipe, and traveled as far as he could with the resources then available to him, to Genoa, some two hundred miles to the north.

But again, he did not stay long. From Genoa he took the road to Turin and then made the journey to Venice. There he found plague and the horror of tens of thousands dead. He moved on again and quickly found another temporary sanctuary in Padua. "Leaving Venice, I went to Padua," Bruno told his judges, ". . . where

---

12. During the Venetian trial, Mocenigo also claimed Bruno had, on many occasions, broken his vows of chastity. It is interesting to note that the Venetian Inquisitors ignored this too, a fact that further supports the notion that they did not want anything tangential to obscure their central concerns.

I found some Dominican fathers of my acquaintance. They persuaded me to wear my habit again, showing me that it was more convenient to travel with than without it. With this idea in my mind, I went to Bergamo and had a robe made of cheap white cloth, and over this I wore the scapular which I had kept with me when I left Rome."[13]

Traveling once more as a monk, Bruno left Padua for Milan, about ninety miles to the northwest. By this time he had been traveling for more than two years and he must have been exhausted and beginning to feel the strain. The itinerant life provided freedom and the chance of adventure, but it was a desperately hard path to follow. He had little money, and roadside accommodations were almost universally appalling. He would have been obliged to stay in filthy inns, sharing cramped, rat-infested rooms with others. His fellow travelers would have been a ramshackle bunch, for anyone with decent money would have stayed somewhere better. In cheap inns, travelers were frequently robbed and many were murdered in their beds or on the straw-covered floor, bludgeoned or knifed for a few pennies or a pair of new boots. And aside from the human threat, plague and a host of other diseases were a constant danger.

But such a life also brought Bruno into contact with a great variety of people. Swapping the isolation and security of the monastery, he now faced danger but also rubbed shoulders with other philosophers and thinkers, traveling musicians, poets and actors, down-at-the-heels merchants and peripatetic preachers. He

13. Doc. ix.

was in touch with the world, and this evidently flowed into his thinking and his writing and provided him with many of the characters that would later people his great books, figures through whom he could expostulate his ideas and philosophies.

In Milan, Bruno met Philip Sidney, the English nobleman and poet who would remain a lifelong friend and to whom Bruno later dedicated his *The Expulsion of the Triumphant Beast*. They were introduced by a group of scholars living in the city, philosophers who bridged the world of the peripatetic occultists, the alchemists, and the heretical monks with that of wealthy travelers and nobility who were known to be interested in clandestine truths and secret cabala. But Milan and this circle were to join the rapidly shifting landscape of Bruno's life, for he stayed there only a week or two before taking the advice of friends and heading for Geneva. Here the Calvinists had made their stronghold and provided sanctuary for Protestant sympathizers and some antipapists.

John Calvin had established his church in Geneva almost forty years before Bruno arrived there. In 1579, Calvin had been in his grave fifteen years, but his influence remained almost undiminished. The city provided a haven for Protestants, who still referred to it as "the City of God," just as they had when Calvin had walked its streets. The largely Protestant population still followed the strict ethical and theological code laid out in Calvin's "Institutes," believing that every action and all life should serve the sole purpose of glorifying God. They scorned most progressive or liberal thinking.

So why would Bruno of all people think of going there of all places? He was quite aware of the fate that had awaited Michael Servetus only a quarter of a century earlier. It seems that for the thirty-one-year-old Bruno, curiosity was a more powerful force than fear. "I often went to hear heretics preach or dispute rather through curiosity as to their ways than because I found them inviting," he told the Venetian judges of his time in Geneva. ". . . Nor had I satisfaction: so that after the reading or sermon, when the time came for the sacrament and the distribution of bread in their style, I went about my business. I have never taken the sacrament or observed their practices."[14]

Inevitably, Bruno soon ran into trouble among the Protestants. With misplaced confidence, he began teaching, and for the first time he openly attacked Aristotle. His judgment was indeed faulty. The Calvinists had reinterpreted the Bible to suit their theological disposition, but in some ways they were every bit as traditional as the Catholics. They remained loyal to Aristotelianism, and like their Catholic enemies, they viewed his philosophy as a central pillar of their theology, a suitable and accurate portrayal of God's physical universe. So Bruno could hardly have been surprised when after publishing a strongly worded anti-Aristotelian tract, he found himself brought before the Church authorities. Yet, according to the city records, Bruno seems to have taken the matter lightly. "Neither did he excuse himself nor plead guilty," the report runs, ". . . for [he claimed] the matter had not been truly reported." The record concludes, "It was decided that he

---

14. Doc. xii.

should be thoroughly reprimanded and allowed to partake of the sacrament. The said reprimand to free him from his transgression; for which he humbly offered thanks."[15]

Apparently on this occasion the city elders were in a forgiving mood, but Bruno was less than inspired by Calvinist ways. He would later write of the philosophers he found in Geneva, "Among ten kinds of teachers there is not to be found one who has not formed to himself a Catechism ready to be published to the world, if not published already, approving no other institution but his own, finding in all others something to be considered, disapproved or doubted of; besides that, the greater part of them disagree with themselves, blotting out today what they had written yesterday."

And before the Venetian court, he declared, "I have read books by . . . Calvin and other heretics, not to acquire their doctrine or for improvement, for I think them more ignorant than myself, but out of sheer curiosity."[16] His curiosity quickly sated, before his luck might turn, Bruno wisely moved on again, this time returning to France, where he took a brief sojourn in Lyon before traveling on to Toulouse.

Again, this was a strange choice. Although the University of Toulouse had a reputation for academic excellence, the city itself was one of the most intolerant in France, staunchly orthodox, dominated by Catholic zealots; it would hardly seem to offer a peaceful haven for Bruno.

---

15. Registres du Consistoire: Vol. de 1577–79, Geneva University Library.
16. Doc. xii.

But we should not be too surprised by Bruno's decision. Indeed, to be puzzled by it is to miss the true essence of his character. For by this time he must have come to see himself as something of a noble fugitive, a crusader. He had been forced to move from city to city, just one step ahead of persecution, and he was beginning to harden to this peripatetic life. He had resisted the persecution of the Calvinists and remained unconvinced by their doctrine, but we must not underestimate the risks he had taken in making such decisions.

Bruno seems to have been drawn to Toulouse by the very fact that it represented a challenge. Disregarding its doctrinal leanings, he began to teach there and became immersed in new work, starting one of his earliest treatises, his first mature study of memory, *Clavis magna* (*The Great Key*). He joined a literary society called the Palace Academy and was soon accepted as a scholar by the university authorities; he was even awarded an official appointment to teach Aristotle. But once again, his heretical ideologies were quickly noticed and he ran into trouble, so that within months of his arrival, he was forced to leave. As he described it to the Venetian Inquisition, "I left on account of the civil wars, and went on to Paris."[17]

Bruno arrived in the French capital late in 1581. He had been traveling for four years and had settled nowhere for longer than a few months. He had little money and few credentials that would hold him in good stead in this divided Catholic city, and still he

---

17. Doc. ix. By "civil wars" he meant the ongoing religious conflict between the Huguenots and the Catholics that had resulted in the St. Bartholomew's Day Massacre of 1572.

was forced to be ever watchful of Vatican spies and agents of the Inquisition. Once more, he had descended into a viper's nest, perhaps the most dangerous place for him outside Italy. By 1581, Paris had been ravaged by almost two decades of religious wars, its streets were ruined, the buildings decaying and misused, the population disproportionately skewed toward women and the old because so many young men had been killed. It was a place where murder was easy and often went unpunished, and provided yet another dismal backdrop for Bruno's odd misanthropy, his desperate, passionate mission.

But within the intellectual circles of Paris, Bruno was already a famous man. His teachings and writings had been judged not only by those who would persecute him; he had made useful inroads into the small but influential community of cabalists and wealthy radicals, curious about the occult and mystic practices. Encouraged by his reception among these people, he began a series of public lectures, which drew the attention of sympathizers at the University of Paris. With surprising speed, he was offered a chair and had soon attracted the attention of King Henry himself. "I got me such a name that King Henry III summoned me one day. . . . He gave me an Extraordinary lectureship with a salary," Bruno reported proudly to the Inquisition.[18]

But once again the good times were not to last; how could they when Bruno was deliberately entering a war zone that had been created by religious conflict? How could he avoid making enemies when he was expostulating in detail and for all to hear his extreme

18. Doc. ix.

views and then, with the support of only a few friends, securing himself academic positions and court favors that gave him a high public profile? He was playing dangerously and parading his fearless heresies; it could not last.

But at first he had enjoyed the protection of the highest power in the land and had formed a close and genuine relationship with Henry. The king was an individualist, a maverick, but not unintelligent. He has been described as a pervert and a hedonist, and by others as an anomaly, a crazed, irresponsible amoralist, and throughout his relatively short life (he died a few weeks before his thirty-eighth birthday) he generated intense reactions from both his own people and foreigners. Bruno was drawn to him perhaps as a fellow traveler on a path less well trodden, and the two men shared a rebelliousness and a taste for the unorthodox. Henry was fortunate enough to have been born into a royal family; with this background he could happily indulge himself. Bruno was a man of very different intellectual caliber but enjoyed none of Henry's privileges. He was a seeker of Truth but chased something starkly different from Henry's pure hedonism. Nevertheless, there was an empathy between the two, and because of this (and for his own ends) Henry was prepared to assist Bruno. He could neither shelter the magus nor be seen to directly support a known heretic, but he did what he could, furnishing him with a letter of recommendation and securing for him accommodation in the home of Michel de Castelnau, Lord of Mauvissière, the French ambassador to the court of Queen Elizabeth in London.

And here the dark trail of Bruno's life fades almost to invisibility. Bruno spent over two years in England, his longest stay in one place since his youth. We know he spent almost all this time in the home of Castelnau at Salisbury Court, close to Fleet Street in Westminster, and was introduced to the English court and to Elizabeth herself. He renewed his friendship with Philip Sidney, who was then at the apogee of his fame and success; he visited Oxford, where he gave public lectures and, as he had done in Toulouse and Paris, gathered the opprobrium of the university dons and many of the students, so that he was all but physically expelled from the city. We also know Bruno wrote his most accomplished and lasting works during his English sojourn. Most prominent was *The Ash Wednesday Supper*, which centers on a drama played out in the streets of Westminster and involving some of the people with whom he had dealings at court and within literary circles.

It is easy to see why Bruno was attracted to England. The country had been cast into turmoil over religious conflict in much the way other parts of Europe had been during the past century, but England was now ruled by a Protestant queen who did not lean toward Calvin and who certainly had no love of Rome (she had been excommunicated by Pope Pius V in 1570). England still seethed with religious confusion, and this would occasionally erupt into violence on all levels and through all strata of society. As Bruno intrigued the intellectual liberals of England with his ideas about mnemonics and his anti-Aristotelian philosophy, Mary Queen of Scots was enduring her final years of captivity in an English castle, and when Bruno left the country, Mary was only two years away from death under the ax at Fotheringhay Castle. Although England had escaped some of the more destructive repercussions of Luther's revolution, the fuse Elizabeth's father, Henry VIII, and her half brother, Edward VI, had lit still smoldered.

Bruno knew all of this, of course, but nevertheless treated England as something of a safe haven while he took stock of his life. However, his connection with the English queen only added to his condemnation by the Inquisition. By the time of Bruno's trial, less than four years after the English had defeated the Spanish Armada, Queen Bess was considered a goddess by her people, but in the eyes of the pope, she was Public Enemy Number One, an excommunicant, a heretic, and a whore. A decade earlier, the Holy See had decreed that anyone who assassinated Elizabeth would not only be forgiven but receive special favor in heaven.

Yet if Bruno's reasons for going to England are obvious, much of his time there is unaccounted for. Convincing evidence now suggests he was a spy for Sir Francis Walsingham, principal secretary to Elizabeth. Bruno was, after all, a man with many European contacts, a man who though ostensibly Catholic held only contempt for the institution of the papacy and the Roman Church authorities. Most important, while he lived at the French ambassador's residence he was perfectly placed to pass on information.[19] According to recent research, during his brief career as a spy Bruno used the pseudonym "Faggot," which, if nothing else, shows he enjoyed a very Anglo-Saxon sense of gallows humor, for a faggot is a bundle of sticks such as would be placed with the tinder at the base of a stake during an execution by fire.

---

19. John Bossy, *Giordano Bruno and the Embassy Affair* (New Haven, Conn., 1991).

Bruno was cosmopolitan and enjoyed a broad circle of friends. At the English court he mixed with the highest echelons of society, but he was also drawn to the streets and continued to network, to liaise with the underworld of alchemists and Hermeticists. This linked him with artists and musicians, poets and actors. He certainly met and discussed magic with the infamous John Dee (one of Elizabeth's spiritual guides), and he made a lasting impression because of his studies in the art of memory.

Bruno left England when he came to realize Elizabeth would not help him and he would be forced to find another way to present his grand schemes. Returning to Paris, he believed he had been away long enough for the memory of his earlier misadventures to have faded sufficiently. In this he was right, and he quickly gathered about him a cadre of influential friends. "I accompanied the Ambassador to Paris, where I stayed another year, boarding and lodging with the gentlemen I knew there," he reported to the Venetian Inquisitors.[20] He continued to teach and to write and was kept busy finding publishers for his new works. But once more voices of opposition were soon raised. In reference to this period, Bruno told his judges, "I have not taught in direct opposition to the Catholic religion, but I was judged to do so indirectly at Paris."

Even so, this was one of the most productive and creative periods of his life. During the three years between his arrival in England in 1583 and his departure for France late in 1585, he wrote seven new books. Some of these have been lost and may never

---

20. Doc. ix.

have been published, but they include four of his most important works: *The Ash Wednesday Supper, The Expulsion of the Triumphant Beast, On the Infinite Universe and Its Worlds,* and *On Cause, Principle and the One.* The first two of these are still in print in English, more than four centuries after their first appearance. But perhaps more important, Bruno now came to realize his chances of securing patronage for his religious crusade were fading fast; both Henry and Elizabeth had rejected his overtures, and France was beginning to find its own form of temporary resolution to the question of religious conflict.

Looking at his contemporaries and their personal missions, their successes and their failures, Bruno must have felt his life's work poised at a crossroads. In terms of trying to reach his audience, Bruno had certainly looked upon Erasmus as a role model and considered his approach a paradigm for his own efforts to effect change. In the style of Erasmus, Bruno had become an exile, unable to have any direct contact with Rome and the Holy Church, ostracized, excommunicated, constantly shadowed by the Inquisition but always just beyond their reach. Bruno had published book after book, expounded his beliefs in inflammatory lectures, and stirred up as much of a reaction as he possibly could everywhere he went. But it had done little. Bruno's success during his lifetime was as nothing compared to the popular reaction to Erasmus. In modern terms, Erasmus's *Moriae encomium (The Praise of Folly)* was a blockbusting best-seller and carried with it massive influence among the educated. By comparison, although treated with respect and in some quarters reverence, Bruno's works were read by few; they were cult successes. So Bruno knew he needed to change course, to try a different tack. The problem was that his work was far more radical than Erasmus's could ever have been, and Bruno knew that genuine change would have to come from the influence of powerful political figures. Having failed twice, he decided it was time for a new approach; he would have to make overtures to the Church.

"I approached the French Nuncio, Monsignor, the Bishop of Bergamo," Bruno told the Venetian court. "Whilst I strove by means of these gentlemen to return to the Church, I consulted another Jesuit; and they told me that they could not absolve me of apostasy. . . . I prayed the Nuncio and sought again earnestly that he would write to His Beatitude, Sixtus V, at Rome, to obtain the grace and be received into the bosom of the Catholic Church, but that I should not be compelled to return to monkdom. Wherefore the Nuncio had no hope and would not write unless I were willing to return to my order. He referred me to the Jesuit father, Alonzo Spagnuolo. I discussed my case with him, and he showed me that it was necessary to procure absolution from censure from the Pope and that nothing could be done unless I went back to my order."[21]

An almost identical offer had been made to every apostate who wished to repent and return to the Church. In 1521, the same offer had been extended to Martin Luther, who wisely chose to stay in Germany. Rome's offer was entirely hollow and Bruno knew it. It was clear to all that a return to the monastery in Naples would mean immediate arrest, imprisonment, torture, and almost

---

21. Doc. xvii and Doc. xi.

certainly execution; few were ever fooled into believing the Holy Roman Church and His Beatitude Sixtus V could be trusted to demonstrate any form of leniency toward heretics.[22]

Of course, Bruno did not say as much to the court. As he delivered his tale during the third day of his trial, May 29, 1592, he reiterated his commitment to finding a way in which he could return to the Church and be accepted for what he was and for what he believed. He reassured his judges that he had never represented any form of threat to the Church, that, on the contrary, he loved the Catholic faith and wanted to glorify it, just so long as he could freely express himself. "I was about to proceed hence to Frankfurt again to get certain of my works printed, especially one on the seven liberal arts, together with other of my printed works, both these which I confirm and those which I do not confirm, and place myself at the feet of His Beatitude (for I have learned that he loves upright men).[23] I desired to explain my case and to try to be absolved for my misbehavior and allowed to wear the clerical habit, but free from monastic authority, whereupon I have spoken during these days to many Neapolitan Fathers of my order

---

22. Some readers may wonder why it is that known heretics like Bruno were not simply taken from wherever they were in Europe and forced to recant or face execution in Rome. Ironically, perhaps, the Church was disinclined toward such methods. The Inquisition always wanted the heretic to come to it willingly and then to piously admit his wrongheadedness for all to see and hear. Before executing a heretic, Inquisitors did everything they could to encourage the victim to recant and to make it known publicly that he had been pursuing false notions before being guided toward the light of truth.

23. The works were *The Trivium* (*On Grammar, Rhetoric and Dialectics*) and *The Quadrivium* (*On Arithmetic, Mathematics, Astronomy and Music*), which together comprised the seven liberal arts Bruno mentions here.

who were here and particularly Father Superior Fra Domenico of Nocera, Father Serafino of Nocera, Father Giovanni, who comes I know not whence, save that it is the Kingdom of Naples, and yet another of Atripalda, who left off his habit but resumed it; I don't know his name; in religion he was called Brother Felice."[24]

But from the moment he first conceived the idea that he might return to the faith yet maintain his idiosyncratic worldview, the response from the clergy was always the same: "Return to Naples or the Vatican itself and the matter may be discussed."

And as Bruno concluded the recounting of this part of his story, his words trailed off into a heavy silence. The room had grown dark around him as his tale had unfolded, candles had been lit, and now shadows flickered across the faces of all around him. Bruno looked at Father Giovanni Gabrielle, at Laurentio Priuli, then across to Ludovico Taberna and Aloysio Fuscari, the assessor, before turning to the gathered observers and witnesses. Father Gabrielle, his face expressionless, rose, and his voice, resonating with power and authority, ordered everyone present to swear silence before he adjourned the trial until the following day. Bruno, exhausted, his face drawn and lined, was returned to his cell.

That evening Bruno received his first visit from one of the Venetian confraternities that took food and provisions to prisons. The best-known was the Fraterne, but two others also worked hard for prisoners, the Scuole and the Corporazioni delle Arti.

---

24. Doc. ix.

These were charitable organizations whose members made personal visits, tended wounds, fed prisoners, and left blankets and medicines. The state felt little obligation to do more than incarcerate those on trial; its only real concern was to prevent escape, and, aside from the aid provided by the confraternities, prisoners relied on help from friends and relatives. Bruno was probably well cared for because he had wealthy and influential associates, but he was also a famous antiestablishment figure who would undoubtedly have been treated especially harshly by the authorities and the cutthroat guards of the prison.[25]

Also that evening, no more than fifty yards from Bruno's dark cell, his judges met in private to discuss, over fine food and free-flowing wine, the problem prisoner whose fate lay in their hands. They were clearly troubled. Gabrielle and Priuli were certainly growing concerned for their position. Rome was desperate for this man, and having heard Bruno's tale, they could understand why. But as Venetians they could not simply hand the man over to the pope, as such a move would attract criticism from many quarters. Venetian patriots would accuse them of weakness, those inclined to religious tolerance would claim they were stoking the fires of

---

25. The Venetian prisons were particularly unpleasant because of overcrowding. Unusually, Bruno was kept in solitary confinement because of the nature of his crimes; the authorities did not want him proselytizing to a captive and impressionable audience.

The year before Bruno's arrest, a farsighted local physician named Giovanni Ottato published an official report that condemned the treatment of prisoners and included a litany of problems with the Venetian prison system, highlighting the incidence of disease among inmates caused by the unsanitary conditions, the poor air, the rat-infested cells, and the substandard diet.

prejudice, and the lawyers might even suggest such a move was illegal. But they were also good Catholics, men who despised heresy. This man Giordano Bruno was obviously dangerous. At the very least they needed more information from him and from others; Mocenigo, they realized, must be forced to provide a third statement immediately. Then, when the court was returned, they must each plumb the depths of this vile individual Bruno, whose sordid views they would expose; they would reveal the limits of his depravity so that no one could doubt what they must do next.

"Bruno believes," Mocenigo claimed in his third report to the Venetian Inquisition, "the Church manifests violence, not love toward heretics. The world could not remain in ignorance and without good religion. Truly the Catholic religion was more acceptable to him than others; but all needed much reform on itself, for it could not continue to corrupt. There is greater ignorance than ever was aforetime, he claimed, since men now teach what they do not understand, namely that God is a Trinity, which is impossible and blasphemous against the Majesty of God. When I told him to be silent and hasten on with what he had to do for me, because I was a Catholic and he a Lutheran, and I could not abide him, he replied, 'Oh, you will see what your faith will do for you,' and laughing, he added, 'wait the Judgment, when the dead shall arise you will get the reward of your righteousness.' And on another occasion, he said, 'This Republic has a reputation for great wisdom; it should deal with the monastic revenues and the friars live on broth. The friars of today are all asses, and to let them enjoy so much wealth is a great sin.' Also, he told me that ladies pleased him well; but he had not yet reached Solomon's number; the Church sinned in making wickedness of that which was of great service in Nature, and which, in his view, was highly meritorious."[26]

The morning after receiving this statement the judges reconvened the trial. First in the chair was a local priest, Father Superior Fra Domenico, in whom Bruno had confided. He told the court, "In this very month of May, on the Holy Feast of the Pentecost, as I was coming out of the Sacristy of the Church of St. John and St. Paul, I observed a layman bow to me. At first I did not know him; but when he spoke to me saying, 'Come into a private place,' I remembered him as one of our brethren in the province of the kingdom, a man of letters, Brother Giordano of Nola by name. We withdrew to a quiet place in the aforesaid church, and there he told me the reason of his leaving our province and of the cause of his unfrocking; being excommunicated by Fra Domenico Vita, provincial at the time. He told me of his sojournings in many Kingdoms and at Royal Courts and of his important work in lecturing, but that he had always lived as a Catholic. And when I asked him what he did in Venice and how he subsisted, he said that he had been in Venice but a very short time and had his own sufficient means; and that he wished to live quietly and set about the writing of a book he had in mind. And then, through important patronage, he would present it to His Beatitude and obtain his pardon together with satisfaction of conscience for what he had to tell me about.

---

26. Doc. viii.

He hoped to stay in Rome, to devote himself to literature, to show what he was made of, and perhaps to deliver some lectures."[27]

The priest completed his statement matter-of-factly; the court seemed rather disappointed, so next the Inquisitors called Bruno before them so that he might continue his story. This he did beginning with his wanderings after leaving France the second time; his journey to Germany, his time at Wittenberg, Prague, and Brunswick between 1586 and 1589, his visit to the Frankfurt book fair, and his initial contact with Giovanni Mocenigo. As Bruno described the letters he had received from Mocenigo, the strain of his incarceration must have been clear for all to see. "I have uttered myself and handled matters too philosophically, wrongly, not sufficiently after the manner of a good Christian, and, in particular, I have taught and maintained in some of these works philosophical doctrines concerning what, according to Christian faith, should be attributed to the power, wisdom, and goodness of God: founding my doctrine on sensible experience and reason and not on faith."[28]

It is difficult to know whether Bruno said this out of fear as a mild form of recantation or whether he was merely musing, reflecting upon what he had done, such thoughts provoked by the telling of his tale. What he is really saying is, Yes, my views are far from official doctrine and you may brand me a heretic, but they have come from long and concentrated philosophizing and dedicated study, and most important they derive from reason rather than faith; this does not mean I'm a bad Catholic.

---

27. Doc. x.
28. Doc. ix.

Yet, it was just the sort of admission the judges were waiting for, the kind of recorded statement that could later be twisted and used against him. But by this time it was too late in the day to embark upon a full-blooded philosophical debate. Gabrielle and Priuli both knew they would need a clear head for such things, and the Father Inquisitor adjourned until Monday, June 2, when Giordano Bruno the heretic would be called upon to give a thorough and clear account of his beliefs.

For the resumption of the trial, the state assessor, Aloysio Fuscari, was replaced by another of the three Venetian *savii all'eresia*, one Sebastian Barbadico, who was sworn in and took his place beside Gabrielle, Laurentio Priuli, and the apostolic nuncio, Ludovico Taberna. Bruno was then brought before them and the questioning resumed.

They began by asking him if he had been involved in occult practices since arriving in Venice. "Never since I have been in Venice have I taught heretical doctrine," he declared, ". . . but have only discussed philosophy with many patricians, as they can tell you. Many patricians and literary people gathered together there [Venice] and I have entered into discussion with some librarians." Then, keeping faith with his new friends, he added guardedly, ". . . but I do not recollect particular persons, for I did not know who they might be."[29]

---

29. Doc. xvii.

This was of course a blatant lie, but the court had no evidence to disprove the statement, only Mocenigo's hearsay and uncorroborated claims. And so the judges moved on quickly. Bruno had been furnished with a complete set of his own works, from which he was allowed to quote, and the Inquisitors began to probe into the man's philosophy and beliefs. And for his part Bruno seemed to find new energy.

"These works," Bruno said, placing a hand on a pile of books beside him, ". . . are purely philosophical and I hold the intellect should be free to inquire provided it does not dispute divine authority but submits to it."[30]

And so here we have the very essence of Bruno's heresy. His views on science and philosophy, even his anti-Aristotelianism, were of secondary importance to the crucial issue, which was that he believed in God but not in Rome. When he declares that the intellect should be given free rein so long as it does not conflict with *divine* authority, he means this in its purest sense. While orthodox Catholics saw no distinction between the word of God and the word of the pope, Bruno most definitely did. He had little respect for the Church establishment and believed each man was answerable only to God Himself. But to the cardinals, such beliefs were quite intolerable.

Even so, Bruno believed he could make the authorities understand him, force them to accept his ideas. In this respect he was either absurdly naive or possessed by his own ego, blind to the realities of human nature and the forces he was facing. At this

30. Doc. vi.

stage, only days into his first trial, he still believed he could convince and persuade, he still held the view that the men sitting across from him in the court and the men at the center of power in the Holy City were cerebral, intelligent people who could surely see that intellect and faith could successfully coexist. Bruno could not identify the animal in his enemy, the devil on the shoulder, the evil in the soul; he still thought intellect could overwhelm fear and prejudice, that greater glory would come to those who supplanted earthly power with the understanding of Truth. He was, of course, utterly wrong and walked into the lion's den barefoot and unarmed.

"I have ever expounded philosophically and according to the principles of Nature and its light; not chiefly considering what must be held according to Faith," he announced bravely. ". . . And I believe that nothing can be found by which I can be judged rather to animadvert on religion than to uphold philosophy; although I may have set forth much impious matter occasioned by my own light . . . never have I taught anything directly contrary to the Catholic Religion, although I was judged to have done so indirectly at Paris, where, indeed, I was allowed to maintain certain discussions entitled: *A Hundred and Twenty Articles against the Peripatetic School and other commonly accepted Philosophers;* and this was printed by permission of the authorities. I was allowed to expound on natural principles without prejudice to truth in the light of faith, in which way one can read and teach the works of Aristotle and Plato; for they are indirectly contrary to the faith in the very same manner—much more so, in fact, than the philosophy I propounded and defended, the whole of which is expounded in my last Latin books published at Frankfurt and entitled *De mi-nimo, De monade,* and *De immenso,* and in part, *De compositione.* In these my object and doctrine may be specifically read, which is, in a word: I hold the universe to be infinite as a result of the infinite divine power; for I think it unworthy of divine goodness and power to have produced merely one finite world when it was able to bring into being an infinity of worlds. Wherefore I have expounded that there is an endless number of individual worlds like our earth. I regard it, with Pythagoras, as a star, and the moon, the planets, and the stars are similar to it, the latter being of end-less number. All these bodies make an infinity of worlds; they constitute the infinite whole, in infinite space, an infinite universe, that is to say, containing innumerable worlds. So that there is an infinite measure in the universe and an infinite multitude of worlds. But this may be indirectly opposed to truth according to the faith."[31]

Bruno had been an eloquent and respected teacher and in the clarity with which he explains his ideas it is easy to see why, but even he must have known that with his final sentence he was mak-ing a considerable understatement. Was he being ironic? Was he deliberately inflaming sentiment, or was he so used to the hetero-dox nature of his worldview he hardly realized what he was saying? Gabrielle, Priuli, and Taberna were learned, well-read men, famil-iar with the heretical statements and ideas of many before Bruno, but this man before them now was not merely dabbling at the

---

31. Doc. ix.

fringes of theology; what he was saying was so far from official doctrine that many would have simply considered Bruno mad.

"Within the universe I place a universal Providence, whereby everything lives, everything grows, acts, and abides in its perfection," he went on. "And I understand this in a twofold way: one, after the fashion of the spirit which is completely present in the whole body and in every part thereof. This I call Nature, the shadow and record of the Divine. The other manner is the inconceivable way in which God, an essence, presence, and power, is in all and above all, not as part, not as spirit, but unspeakably.

"Now I understand all attributes to be one and the same in Deity, and, with theologians and the greatest thinkers, I conceive of three attributes: power, wisdom, and goodness; or, mind, comprehension, and Love. Things are through mind, they are ordered and are distinct through intellect; they are in harmonious proportion through universal love, in all and above all. There is nothing that doth not shine in being, any more than anything is beautiful without the presence of beauty; wherefore nothing can exist shorn from the divine presence. But distinctions in the Divinity are made by the method of Discursive Thought and are not reality."[32]

He then went on to describe how he concurred with Aristotle on the matter of a First Cause, a moment of Creation, after which he tried rather unconvincingly to marry his philosophy with the doctrine of the Holy Trinity, linking the Father to Will or Power; the Son, or the Word, to the Intellect; and the Holy Spirit to Love,

---

32. Doc. xi.

and he added, "All things, souls and bodies, are immortal as to their substance, nor is there any other death than dispersion and reintegration."[33]

Unsatisfied, the Inquisitors continued to probe. Did he then hold the Trinity to be only in Essence but distinct Persons? they wanted to know.

This was a direct challenge. Bruno equivocated. "What is 'Person'?" he asked. "According to St. Augustine, the word was new in his age."

"Had you then doubted the existence of the One, the existence of God?" came the reply.

"Never," Bruno retorted forcefully.

"And what of Christ and the incarnation, was that then a lie?" came the angry response.

"I have doubted and wrestled with this matter; I have never denied the dogma, only doubted." Bruno declared, ". . . And I believe the Father and Son are one in essence."[34] Again, naturally resisting open heresy, he added that as a youth he had only *quoted* the ideas of Arius. "I showed the view of Arius to be less dangerous than it was commonly taken to be," he announced. "For it was generally understood that Arius meant to teach that the Word was the first creation of the Father; and I explained that Arius said the Word was neither Creator nor created, but intermediate between the Creator and the creature, just as the spoken word is the intermediary between the speaker and the meaning he sets forth."[35]

33. Doc. xii.
34. Doc xi.
35. Doc. xiii.

"To make clearer what I have said," he went on, "I have held and believed that there is a distinct Godhead in the Father, in the Word, and in Love, which is the Divine Spirit; and in Essence, these three are one; but I have never been able to grasp the three really being Persons and have doubted it. Augustine says: 'We utter the name of Person with dread when we speak of divine matters, and use it because we are obliged.' Nor have I found the term applied in the Old or New Testament."[36]

Continuing with their line of questioning on the details of doctrine, the Inquisitors asked Bruno to explain his thoughts on the incarnation. In response, he told them he could not understand how the finite flesh of humanity could be fused with the Word, an infinite essence, but accepted that Christ had incarnated on earth, seeing him more as a *representative* of God rather than one with God. He accepted miracles as an expression of divinity and respected the Church doctrine of transubstantiation. Why else had he never partaken of the sacrament after he was excommunicated?

Without mentioning the source of the claim, Father Gabrielle then repeated Mocenigo's accusation, that he, Bruno, had denied Christ's divinity, and had declared the Son of God to be an "evil wretch."

Bruno appeared genuinely stunned by this. "I marvel that you should ask such a question," he declared. "Never did I say or think such a thing about Christ. I believe as Holy Mother Church does about him."

---

36. Ibid.

According to the clerk of the court, Bruno then appeared hurt, mournful, saying, "I cannot conceive how such things could be imputed to me. I hold that Christ was begotten, by the Spirit, of a Virgin-mother. If this be shown false I shall submit to any penalty. . . . I have repeatedly tried to be absolved and accepted by the Church. I have held and still hold the immortality of souls which are kinds of existence especially due to substance. That is to say, speaking Catholically, the intellectual soul does not pass from body to body, but goes to Paradise, Purgatory, or Hell; but I have thought deeply, as a Philosopher, how, since the soul does not exist without body and does not exist in the body, it may pass from body to body even as matter may pass from mass to mass," Bruno concluded.[37]

"And so you are a skilled theologian and acquainted with Catholic decisions, are you?" Gabrielle asked.

Bruno was taken aback. "Not much," he replied. "I have pursued philosophy, which has been my avocation."

"Have you then criticized theologians?"

"No, I have not. I have read Protestant teachings and always argued for Catholic doctrine, especially the teachings of Aquinas. I have read heretical books and dissected them. Read my work, it is there."

"Have you mocked priests and monks?"

Exasperated, Bruno threw up his arms. "I have said nothing of the kind, nor held that view."[38]

---

37. Doc. xi.
38. Doc. xiv.

The judges then went through Mocenigo's accusations one by one, and Bruno deflected each, sometimes with irritation, occasionally with stark disbelief. He was growing increasingly agitated; the judges could see it and they exploited it.

"Do you believe Christ wrought his miracles by magic?" Father Gabrielle asked.

Bruno threw up both hands and looked bewildered. "What is this?" he cried. "Who invented these devilries? I have never thought such a thing. Oh God! What is this? I would rather be dead than have said anything of the kind."

The judges then raised the subject of Bruno's work on the art of memory, suggesting this was an occult practice. "You are a known occultist," Gabrielle declared. "What of your relationship to the French king?"

"When I was in the court of King Henry," Bruno replied, "he summoned me one day to discover from me if the memory which I possessed was natural or acquired by magical art. I satisfied him that it did not come from sorcery but from organized knowledge."[39]

The judges then pressed him on the nature of the books Mocenigo had taken from him the previous week. "And what of the books you are known to have read? Occult works, the works of heretics?" asked the Father Inquisitor.

Sensing danger, Bruno skirted the issue. "I have indeed seen condemned works such as those of Raymond Lully and other

---

39. Doc. ix.

writers who treat of philosophical matters. I scorn both them and their doctrines," he lied.[40]

"Nonsense," said Gabrielle. "What of the manuscripts found on your person when you were arrested?" Then he looked down at his notes. "What of . . . *The Seals of Hermes?*"

"Indeed, my copyist Herman Besler was at the time making reproductions of ancient, unpublished works, including a work called *The Seals of Hermes*," Bruno responded. "I know I was philandering with perilous material, but I did not see too closely into the contents of these books, and I have not read *The Seals of Hermes*."[41]

Gabrielle was unconvinced but decided to change tack. "You have mocked the faith," he declared. Then, quoting Mocenigo, he added: "'. . . await the Judgment, when the dead shall arise you will get the reward of your righteousness.' Are these not your words?"

Bruno looked stunned. "I have never said these things. My lord, look through my books. They are profane enough; but you will not find a trace of this; nor has it entered my head."[42]

A sudden hush fell over the room; the judges sat motionless. Bruno, his confidence clearly ebbing away, his energy almost

---

40. Doc. xii. Raymond Lully, or Ramon Lull as he was more usually known, was a key character in the alchemical and magical culture of Europe during the early fourteenth century and was imprisoned in the Tower by King Edward III, who demanded he stay in chains until he produced gold to finance a crusade. Bruno may have begun calling Lull Lully after his own spell in England. Bruno often wrote about Lull's work and delivered a series of lectures at Oxford and Paris on what he called "Lullian philosophy."
41. Doc. xiv.
42. Ibid.

drained, looked around the room once more, seeing the still faces, the eyes of witnesses quickly averted. Then the Father Inquisitor spoke.

"You have admitted enough to make the charges against you credible," he declared icily. "You deny the authority of Rome, you question the Trinity, deny the Divinity of Christ, you dispute theology, mock the Mother Church and the priesthood, you lend support to the faithless and practice magic. You must take heed and make full, open, and faithful confession in order to be received into the bosom of the Holy Mother Church and be made a member of Jesus Christ. But it would be a marvel indeed if persistence in your obstinate denial did not lead to the usual end. The Holy Office desires only to bring forth light to the heretic by its Christian love, to bring them from their evil ways and guide them onto the path of eternal life."

The words fell into the silence like lead in water. Bruno kept his head bowed throughout Gabrielle's statement. Then, lifting his head, he said slowly, "So may God pardon me. Every one of my answers to every question has been true so far as my memory has served me; but, for my greater satisfaction, I will again pass my life in review, and, if I have said or done anything against the Catholic Christian Faith, I will frankly confess it. I have said what is just and true, and I shall continue to say it. I am certain the contrary shall never be proved against me."[43]

Rising, Father Gabrielle adjourned the trial until the following day.

---

43. Doc. xiv.

If Bruno had not realized it already, then that night, alone in his cell, he must have come to understand the gravity of what had happened. Gabrielle's words meant only one thing: the Church would punish him. In its inimitable way it wished to redirect the mind and the soul of the heretic by forcing a recantation; then it would imprison him, torture him, and almost certainly burn him. Even the ever optimistic, ever determined Bruno must now have come to understand that this would be his fate.

Next morning, June 3, 1592, Bruno was once more called upon to give evidence. The accusations were read to him again and he was asked if he conceded guilt. "Wherein I have erred, I have told the truth, and you will never find that is not so." Concerning the divinity of Christ in particular, he declared, "What I have held, I have told you, I never talked on the subject."[44] Again, pressed on his views about occult practices, he declared contempt for the art but confessed to an interest in "judicial astrology."

Question after question was a repeat of those asked the previous day, the same ground covered again and again. Finally, Gabrielle asked: "Do you now consider your heresies fallacious?" Bruno replied evenly. "I hate and detest all the errors I have at any time committed as regards the Catholic Faith and decrees of the Holy Church, and I repent having done, held, said, believed, or doubted anything Catholic. I pray this Holy Tribunal that, aware of my infirmity, it will admit me into the bosom of the Church, providing me with remedies proper to salvation and showing mercy."[45]

---

44. Doc. xvii.
45. Ibid.

And with that, the case was adjourned for three weeks, Bruno was taken back to his cell to consider what he had said while the judges considered his fate.

Gabrielle, Priuli, and Taberna met again that evening. What were they to make of this man? At times he had tried to present himself as a devout Catholic who had merely strayed from the core of orthodoxy, renouncing any interest in magic, even denying his learning and understanding, let alone his own contribution to the Hermetic tradition. Yet elsewhere in his testimony, he expressed doubts about central tenets of the Catholic faith.

But they knew Bruno was a skilled performer. He had been a greatly admired lecturer, a polished speaker who had always reveled in attention. He had employed a common trick, to try to speak of heresy almost in the third person, to discuss these things as though they were merely academic, detached entirely from faith.[46] Furthermore, he had been clearly thrilled by the attention, even though the Inquisitors had succeeded in terrifying him. But what could they make of his constantly shifting arguments? What

---

46. During this era, such "double-think" was a very common technique employed by anyone who had dealings with ecclesiastic authorities. Such arguments had rescued the philosopher Pietro Pomponazzi, who in 1516 had written a treatise, *De immortalitate animae*, in which he pointed out that the immortality of the soul could not be confirmed using Aristotelian logic. By successfully convincing his judges that he was speaking purely philosophically and that his reasoning had no impact upon theology, he spared himself the stake. Early in Bruno's hearing, he had similarly claimed that what he said was "according to natural principles and natural understanding, being in no way concerned with that which principally must be maintained according to faith."

did he really believe? How far would he go? What was important to him and what was not?

Clearly, he had lied when he professed to abhor the mystical arts. He had written much on the subject, taught a memory system based upon Hermetic imagery and ancient pre-Christian religious symbolism. They had his books before them. Obviously his interest in such things was never tempered by any guilt, and he was not a man to fear where he trod; to him Christianity was certainly no sacred cow. He had constantly veered close to confession and then pulled back; with this he had been far from subtle. The very notion that he owned occult books but had not read them was quite ridiculous. He had also been circumspect concerning his involvement with the Venetian booksellers and other known occultists in the city. Gabrielle, Priuli, and Taberna knew these men well, for they had been observed from afar; many were marked men, and the scent of the pyre hung about them too.

So, if he could lie about these things, the judges mused, what other sins had he committed? Was everything Mocenigo had written indeed true? The prisoner claimed he believed in the divinity of Christ, but renounced the orthodox meaning of the Trinity. He accepted the idea that Christ performed miracles, but viewed Jesus as only a representative of God rather than an expression of the Trinity. Most important, he insisted upon placing intellect above faith. He was not a man to accept anything without thinking about it first. Dangerous, very dangerous.

But beyond this, what did this man want? He had claimed repeatedly his wish to be absolved and allowed to preach his idiosyncratic doctrine, but why then cast doubt upon the fact of the Holy Trinity? Was he, they wondered, always to remain an enigma?

And so the final days of the Venetian trial began. Three weeks after the last gathering, the Inquisitors met again, this time with a new state representative, Thomas Morosini. On this occasion, Bruno was present but not questioned. Instead, a distinguished scholar and friend of Bruno's, Andrea Morosini, was called to give witness.[47]

With necessary caution, Morosini (who was known to be a dedicated Catholic but also a man interested in occult matters) told the court, "For some months past certain philosophical books had been on sale at Venetian booksellers, bearing the name of Giordano Bruno, a man reputed to be of varied learning. I understood from what I heard in Venice and from what Giovanni Battista the bookseller said to diverse gentlemen, and especially to myself, that this man was here and that we might desire to get him to our house, where certain gentlemen and also prelates are wont to come for the discussion of literature and above all of

---

47. Morosini is a very common and ancient Venetian name. Famous admirals, generals, and merchants and no fewer than five doges had shared this surname. The scholar Andrea Morosini and the politician Thomas Morosini were only distantly related. Andrea Morosini had an illustrious career as a scholar at the University of Padua and as Venetian ambassador. In 1600 he became a senator and five years later joined the highest echelon of government, the *collegio dei savii* (cabinet of ministers).

philosophy. Wherefore I said that he should get him to come; and he did so several times, debating on various learned matters. I have never been able to infer from his reasoning that he held any opinion contrary to the faith, and, so far as I am concerned, I have always considered him to be a Catholic—and at the least suspicion of the contrary, I should not have allowed his presence in my house."[48]

Next Ciotto was called upon again and questioned about what he viewed to be Bruno's intentions. Ciotto reported that Bruno had told him, as he had told others, that he wished to be allowed to return to the Church. Then Ciotto added, "He wished to meet personally with His Holiness in Rome to present to him his latest work."[49]

The next day, June 26, Bruno made his final appearance before the Venetian judges. A second assessor had been called upon for this, the final questioning of the prisoner along with the closing statements of the Inquisitors. Bruno was again reminded of the seriousness of the charges brought against him and the grave suspicions of the Holy See. Asked again if he had, upon solitary reflection, decided to change his testimony or to add any further comment, Bruno repeated that he had been entirely truthful in his statements. "I can understand that my writings and confessions could provoke charges of heresy," he declared, "but I have always felt remorse and harbored the desire to return to the Church. I

---

48. Doc. xv.
49. Doc. xvi.

have never intended any slight to the Faith and have held back through fear of the Holy See and the love of liberty."

But, snatching upon this, Gabrielle retorted, "Had your desire been sincere you would not have lived so long in France and other Catholic countries and here in Venice without having consulted some prelate; whereas you went on teaching false and heretical doctrine up to now."

"But," said Bruno, ". . . my disposition shows I did consult with Catholic Fathers. I have behaved without fault in this city. I have discussed philosophy only, before you I have condemned Protestants. I only wish to live freely uncloistered in my native home. Mocenigo is the only man who could have accused me of the things you claim against me; he is a wicked man. I have searched my conscience for faults and can find none. I have readily confessed everything I know." Then, throwing himself to the floor, prostrate before the Inquisitors, Bruno sobbed, "I humbly demand pardon of God and the Court. I wish only that my punishment be conducted in private so that I may not draw attention to the habit I wear."[50]

Gabrielle told him to rise and asked if there was any final thing he wished to confess. Bruno shook his head in silence. The other judges rose, Bruno was taken roughly from the court to retrace a now familiar journey to his cell, and the officials left to once more discuss the case over a lavish meal.

For Bruno, the point of crisis was approaching fast. It is clear

---

50. Doc. xvii.

the Venetian Inquisitors had been in direct communication with Rome. Short of lying, how else could they have claimed before the court that the pope and the Holy Office were so suspicious of Bruno? And as they dined in Father Gabrielle's rooms, some three hundred miles away in the Vatican others were also talking about the heretic Bruno: the pope's personal representative, the Father Inquisitor, Cardinal Santoro di Santa Severina, was reviewing the Venetian case.

· VI ·

WRANGLES WITH ROME

As America's mental courage is so indebted, above all current lands and peoples, to the noble army of old-world
martyrs past, how incumbent on us that we clear those
martyrs' lives and names, and hold them up for reverent
admiration as well as beacons. And typical of this and
standing for it and all perhaps, Giordano Bruno may well
be put, today and to come, in our New World's thank-
fulest heart and memory.

—Walt Whitman

CARDINAL SEVERINA WAS keen on murder and mutila-
tion. When he heard of the massacre of the Parisian Huguenots in 1572, he called it "a famous and a very joyous day," and
when he was not scheming for promotion in Rome, he traveled
Italy persecuting entire communities, torturing and killing. But
initially at least, he could not bully the Venetians. In response to
the news from Venice that Bruno's trial had ended, he called for a
Congregation of the Roman Inquisition, which, as number two in
the Vatican, he would chair.

The Congregation met on September 12, 1592, and it quickly
decided to do its utmost to persuade Venice to release the prisoner
into its hands; Bruno was a self-confessed heretic who sought to

establish a rival theology to that of Rome and must be dealt with under ecclesiastic law overseen by the Holy Office itself. A letter was prepared and sent to the Venetian *collegio* in which Severina asked for Bruno the heretic to be handed over to the reverend governor of Ancona, who would escort the prisoner under guard to Rome.[1] The letter arrived in Venice on September 17 and was read before the Venetian Inquisition by the state assessor, Thomas Morosini.

It came as little surprise, but the Venetian Inquisitors continued to act with caution. They knew they could not extradite Bruno without the official and personal sanction of the doge and were aware of the politically sensitive nature of the situation. So they waited for the next post from Rome, and several days later a second, more insistent letter arrived. After this was read to the Sacred Tribunal of the Inquisition on September 28, a delegation consisting of a representative of Father Gabrielle of Saluzzo and Thomas Morosini then met with the doge, Pasquale Cicogna, who was accompanied by the governing council in a *collegio dei savii* (a cabinet meeting of the Venetian Republic). The demands from Rome were reported and the Father Inquisitor explained the details of the case.

"Bruno," he declared, ". . . is no simple heretic, but a leader of heretics, an organizer and rebel. He has consorted with Protestants, he is an apostate monk who has openly praised the heretic queen Elizabeth of England and has written occult works that attempt to undermine the sanctity of the Church. I urge the coun-

---

1. Doc. xviii.

cil to act with all haste in this matter. We have a boat ready to transport the prisoner immediately if you approve of this action."

But Pasquale Cicogna was unmoved by the Father Inquisitor's statement. In no mood to be told what to do by the pope, he flatly refused to be rushed into a decision.

"I will give the matter due consideration," he replied firmly, and as the representatives of the Inquisition left, he pointedly turned his attention to other matters.[2]

Like other recent doges, Cicogna had watched with alarm as the Vatican, still recoiling from the Reformation, had made renewed efforts to reforge the temporal power of the Church as well as to bolster its spiritual monopoly. Recent popes had poured money and resources into military conquests and had acquired valuable new territory. Admittedly, Rome was at that moment an ally of Venice, but politics being the way they were in the Peninsula, this could change at any moment, almost without warning. Cicogna knew he had to tread a fine line, to act with diplomacy but to retain national honor.

The afternoon of his meeting with the council, the Father Inquisitor returned to the chamber and asked if the council had reached a decision about the heretic. It had not, the matter being a grave one, and with other pressing government business to deal with, the council and the doge had deferred any further discussion of the matter until a more appropriate time.[3]

More days passed and the Inquisitors heard nothing from the

2. Doc. xix.
3. Doc. xx.

council, but behind the scenes there were clandestine moves concerning the fate of Giordano Bruno. On October 10, a letter dated October 7 was received in Rome by the Venetian ambassador, Luigi Donato, declaring that the papal request concerning Giordano Bruno could not be complied with, as it would infringe upon the rights of the Venetian Inquisition and establish an unacceptable precedent. It concluded with a request that the ambassador should convey this news with his compliments to the Papal Office.[4] Donato replied the same day and stated that he would do all he could to pass this message on with due diplomacy and that if there was to be any argument, he would deal with the matter as best he could.[5]

It is clear from this that the council decided to use the Venetian Inquisition as a buffer, to pass the responsibility for the decision on to it rather than to involve the state in a political wrangle over the heretic imprisoned in the city. And at first this seems to have worked; the Venetian government heard nothing more on the matter of Bruno for a full three months, during which the prisoner remained in isolation, ostensibly ignored.

Then, three days before Christmas, 1592, the affair resurfaced. The apostolic nuncio spoke again at a private meeting of the Venetian Inquisition and repeated the charges brought against Bruno. He pointed out that the man was not a Venetian but a Neapolitan and had been charged with heresy in both Naples and Rome many years earlier. He added that many other cases of

---

4. Doc. xxi.
5. Doc. xxii.

heresy had been referred from the Venetian court to the Holy Roman Tribunal during recent years and that it should be remembered that the Roman court was the most senior of the ecclesiastical authorities. He reinforced his argument by reiterating the vile nature of Bruno's crimes and declaring that although the Venetian authorities could be expected to deal comfortably with general everyday processes, Bruno's was such a serious case it had to be dealt with by none other than the Holy Office itself.

On that day, Donato returned to Venice with a report of his meeting with the pope. According to the ambassador, Clement had been happy to let Venice deal with Bruno, but Severina had intervened personally and forcefully. It was he who had dispatched the nuncio to speak again with the Venetian Inquisition and to once more raise the matter with the doge and his council.[6] Hearing this, the nuncio was recalled and told curtly that the *collegio dei savii* would in due course confer and that it would give the request of His Holiness every consideration. This response was then immediately passed on to an impatient Cardinal Severina in Rome.

By this point, it was becoming obvious to the doge and his council that the irritating problem of Giordano Bruno was simply not going to fade away; a politically expedient solution would have to be found. But what were they to do? On the one hand, they did not want to provoke the pope into a damaging response over a single heretic. On the other, the council had to consider its image before the people of Venice; the important issue of national pride could not be ignored.

6. Doc. xxiii.

Eventually an answer was found, not by the council but by a lawyer, the most famous Venetian advocate of the time, Federigo Contarini, a man renowned for his creativity and subtlety. Devoid of ideas and desperate to find a way through the dangerous political confusion Bruno had created, the council had called upon Contarini in January 1593. It did not take him long to solve their problem.

Contarini sifted through the testimony, the witness statements, and the background to the Bruno trial, as well as the material in dispute, Bruno's heretical writings. Before the Inquisition, Contarini reported that Bruno had "consorted with heretics, that he had escaped to England, where he lived after the fashion of that island, and afterward in Geneva, leading apparently a licentious and diabolical life. But Bruno had," Contarini admitted, "a mind as excellent and rare as one could wish for, and is of exceptional learning and insight. Yet, his heretical offenses are very grave."

Of course, there was nothing new in this statement. The officials in Venice already knew all they could hope to discover about Bruno's "apparently . . . licentious and diabolical life," and arguments over the man's ideas would lead them nowhere in a clash with the Holy Office. But from the material available to him, Contarini had also quickly stumbled upon a possible loophole in the case, one that might disentangle the Venetian government from the mess and appease any public objections.

Blinded perhaps by religious zeal and bigotry, the Inquisition had, Contarini pointed out, overlooked two glaringly obvious facts. First, Bruno was not a Venetian citizen and therefore should not have expected the protection of Venice in the first place;

second, and most important to the commercially obsessed Venetians, Bruno had been selling his books in Venice without paying taxes. In conclusion, Contarini made one further contribution. "The accused has continually asked to be accepted back into the bosom of the Church and has declared his intention to petition His Holiness directly. Why should this state prevent him in his avowed desire?"[7]

Contarini's was a brilliant piece of legal scheming and came as something very sweet indeed to the doge and council, not to mention the frustrated Venetian Inquisition. Interestingly, Contarini concluded his delivery with a request that his part in the process remain secret from the public. The most likely reason for this is that the lawyer had useful contacts among the intelligentsia of Venice—men whom Bruno had befriended and who would not be so readily convinced of the solution Contarini had found for the problem of Giordano Bruno.

After conferring and discussing what Contarini had offered, the council recalled the nuncio, and through him a personal message was sent to Rome. "Due to the exceptional circumstances of the case," it said, ". . . the heretic Bruno shall be delivered over to the nuncio." The same day another letter was sent from the council to the Venetian ambassador in Rome, ordering him to make as much political capital from the arrangement as possible and declaring that the happy outcome of this dispute served only to strengthen the bond between Venice and His Beatitude.[8]

---

7. Doc. xxiv.
8. Doc. xxv.

But for Giordano Bruno, Contarini's cleverness served only to remove him from the one territory in Italy in which he might have had a chance of freedom and the opportunity to pursue his dreams unmolested. The following day, the prisoner was taken from his cell, clamped in irons, and transported under maximum security by sea to Ancona. From there, by horse, Bruno made his final journey along a fork of the Flaminian Way and on to Rome, where the Vatican prisons had been made ready for his arrival.

· VII ·

BLOOD ON THE FLOOR, FIRE IN THE SOUL

The procedure which the Church uses today is not that which the Apostles used: for they converted the people with preaching and the example of a good life, but now whoever does not wish to be a Catholic must endure punishment and pain, for force is used and not love; the world cannot go on like this, for there is nothing but ignorance and no religion which is good.

—Giordano Bruno

A S BRUNO WAS taken across the Tiber running through the heart of the eternal city, he would have caught a view of the cylindrical bulk of the Castel Sant'Angelo. He had seen it before, during his first visit to the city sixteen years earlier. Perhaps he had recalled the stories told to every good Catholic child—how after a terrible plague in 590 the then pope, Gregory the Great, had a vision of Archangel Michael alighting on top of the turret of the castle and sheathing his sword. To Gregory, this vision had signaled the end of the plague, and from it the bleak, ugly monolith gained its name. For centuries, the Castel Sant'Angelo had been a place of refuge for the pious and home of unimaginable pain for the sinner and the heretic. Pope Clement VII barracked himself within the walls when Rome was sacked by Hapsburg troops in 1527, only sixty-six years before Bruno's arrival there, and for over one thousand years, every important prisoner of the Vatican had been incarcerated within its three-foot-thick walls, for this was the home of the prisons of the Inquisition.

The dungeons of the Roman Inquisition were notorious even for the time, and today they still retain an element of horror. Within, the darkness is all-pervading; you can imagine long-ago cries of agony that once resounded through the passageways that link tiny low-ceilinged, dank chambers. The dark atmosphere of such a place exaggerates fear, heightens awareness, and nourishes inner demons; this is an aspect of its power. If you walk through these rooms today, there is always the surety that after a few more turns in the corridor you will be out in the light once again, breathing the charmed air of freedom. For those cast into darkness here by the Inquisition, there was no such reassurance.

And then, as if the claustrophobia, the smell, and the cloying ghosts are not enough, beyond a dozen identical chambers and along a narrow corridor you emerge into a high-ceilinged chamber twenty feet square. Around the walls hang ropes and wires. To one side lies a blackened grate, and set in the walls seven feet above the ground there are foot-wide cast-iron rings. And here you can almost taste blood on your tongue. If you close your eyes, you may catch a whiff of singed flesh, hear the screams of agony. In this chamber the wall rings found continuous use and a fire burned constantly in the grate. Here may be found the very heart of darkness, the epicenter of Christian evil, the torture chamber of the Roman Inquisition.

What little of these rooms was known by the innocent faithful sent ice-cold fingers of fear along spines; for anyone, anyone at all, could be unlucky enough to find himself stretched upon the rack or chained to a wall ring and facing a white-hot poker. But even the Inquisition had grades of punishment, fine divisions of persecution. For those convicted of relatively insignificant crimes against the Church and those who had repented fully, there was the *murus largus,* the "wide wall" or ordinary prison. Here prisoners were allowed to meet and to talk, and they were allowed gifts from the outside, including food to supplement the meager rations provided by the state. But for those found guilty of more serious offenses or under sentence of extreme heresy who found themselves under the turrets of the Castel Sant'Angelo, there was a far more punitive regime, the *murus strictus,* or "narrow wall." Here the prisoner was kept in solitary confinement twenty-four hours a day and had to make do with a virtual starvation diet, which, in the words of one of the Inquisition's founding fathers, Bernard Gui, consisted of "the bread of suffering and the water of tribulation." And in extreme cases there was an even harsher system, the *murus strictissimus,* what may be thought of as a "super-dungeon" in which the prisoner was chained by the wrists and ankles. No one was allowed into the cell and food was passed through a slit in the door. This form of imprisonment was reserved for those convicted of the most heinous crimes against the Church.

Bruno was placed in the middle category. We know this from

the evidence of a few surviving scraps of documents in which he is reported asking for food. As in the Venetian system, in these dungeons prisoners relied upon donations of food from friends or family on the outside or from charitable brotherhoods that were allowed occasional visits to the citadel. But even then the great majority of supplies ended up furnishing the tables of guards and officials and very little made it through to the prisoner. It is hardly surprising then that many guests of the Inquisition died of starvation even before they could be adequately tortured.

Yet, true to their desire to portray an image of humane discipline, the Roman Inquisition had very strict rules guiding the torturer's hand. Manuals containing detailed instructions for the Inquisitor had been produced by the Papal Inquisition as early as the thirteenth century, and these were used until the practice was finally made illegal four centuries later. "Torture," the manual recorded, ". . . should be conducted in accordance with the conscience and will of the appointed judges, following law, reason, and good conscience. Inquisitors should take great care that the sentence of torture is justified and follows precedent."[1] But because all the proceedings of the Inquisition were carried out in absolute secrecy, no one knows precisely what horrors were perpetrated in the name of the Lord.

And the Inquisitors were indeed deft at bending the rules. The manual stipulated that no prisoner could be tortured in the same way more than once. But this presented only a minor, temporary hurdle, for it was soon realized that if the Inquisitor wished to

---

1. Bernard Gui, *Manuel de l'inquisiteur,* trans. G. Mollat (Paris, 1969).

repeat a torture, it was merely recorded as a *continuation* of the previous session.

In the early days of the Inquisition, priests were forbidden to torture because it was impossible for the pope to then allow them to tender the spiritual needs of the laity; instead clerics were present only in a supervisory role and professional torturers were employed. But in 1256, Pope Alexander IV came to the conclusion that if each torture session was attended by at least *two* priests, they could dispense with the hired hand and afterward absolve each other—even after committing the most diabolical physical abuses. The Bull ordered: "Provincials of the Mendicant Orders to assign two or more companions to the inquisitors specifically for the task of absolving them from any *irregularities* they may meet during the course of their work."

A further stipulation from the manual was that the prisoner must not be made to bleed. The reason for this is obscure but seems to derive from the idea that if a prisoner was cut and bled profusely, he might identify himself with Christ and thereby derive an inner strength from the act. It is also possible that by assiduously avoiding the shedding of blood the Inquisitors believed they were distancing themselves from any possible link to Christ's persecutors and torturers who shed the Lord's blood during the crucifixion. Whatever the derivation of this perverse form of self-restraint, it merely meant a little more imagination was required of the torturer; they had to devise forms of abuse that caused maximum pain but kept the body of the victim more or less intact.

The ordeal of water involved forcing a prisoner to consume large quantities of water, usually through a funnel but sometimes through a rag stuffed into the mouth. A variation upon this theme required blocking the prisoner's nose and allowing water to drip slowly into the throat, thus producing the effect of drowning. The Inquisitor would then let the prisoner catch his breath before starting again immediately and continuing until a confession was obtained.

Ordeal by fire was a favorite of the Inquisitors. The prisoner, bound along the length of his body, would be placed in front of a roaring fire. After coating the prisoner's feet with grease, the Inquisitor moved the victim close to the flames so his feet fried. A protective screen could then be placed in front of the fire to give the prisoner a chance to talk, but removed again if the confession was deemed insufficient.

With the *strappado*, or pulley torture, the prisoner had his ankles and wrists bound behind his back. He was then hoisted to the ceiling by a sturdy rope and left to hang for as long as the Inquisitor chose. Then, without warning, a lever was pulled, the rope ran free, and the prisoner fell. But the rope contained just enough slack to bring the prisoner to a violent halt a foot or two above the floor. Like bungee-jumping without elastic, this caused multiple dislocations and extreme pain.

The wheel was one of the earliest forms of torture employed by the Inquisition and one of the most popular. It was still in use among Catholic extremists in the West Indies as late as 1761. In its mildest form, the prisoner, once strapped to the wheel by hands and feet, was subjected to repeated whipping, but if a confession remained elusive the torturers resorted to using iron bars to shatter knees and fracture limbs.

The most famous of all the Inquisitor's techniques was the rack, an ingenious device that slowly stretched the body of the unfortunate prisoner. According to the responses of the victim, the Inquisitor allowed the rollers at each end to move at his chosen speed, pulling muscles and ligaments until, in extreme cases, limbs would be wrenched from sockets and bodies stretched to the point of dismemberment, when internal bleeding would lead to a slow, agonizing death.

The final form of torture was reserved for the most persistently stubborn prisoners and the worst heretics. The *strivaletto* or *brodequin* consisted of four pieces of sturdy wood bound to the ankles with strong rope. The Inquisitor forced wooden wedges between the planks and the ankles of the prisoner, hammering them in with a mallet. In extreme cases, when the prisoner continued to withhold information, up to eight such wedges could be hammered into place until the ropes cut deep into the legs and the bones of the ankles imploded.

Often prisoners confessed before they were tortured, for the mere sight of the implements and a detailed description of what was about to be done were understandably terrifying enough. But some victims were remarkably resistant, or their confessions constantly deemed inadequate. In these cases, the Inquisitors used intimidation and the powerful psychological device of keeping the prisoner in a state of seemingly endless suspense. By continually delaying the torture and allowing the prisoner time to reflect upon the horrors awaiting him, the Inquisitors could often obtain the information they wanted. More often than not they then tortured the hapless prisoner with fire, water, and rope anyway.

Some popes made genuine attempts to control the practices of the Inquisition. In 1306, Clement V had ordered an inquiry into the Inquisitors' use of torture, and his successor, John XXII, passed legislation limiting its practice. In a papal decree of 1317 he insisted upon the addition to the rules which stated, "Torture should be used only with mature and careful deliberation." Whatever John's intention, the addition unfortunately meant nothing and achieved less. John then issued a further instruction stipulating that before he could subject a prisoner to torture, an Inquisitor must obtain the agreement of the bishop of a province so long as it could be obtained within eight days.

Many senior members of the Inquisition objected strongly to this. The senior Inquisitor Bernard Gui was particularly vociferous in his criticism of the rule, claiming that it would greatly impede the work of the Inquisition. But this was an overreaction, for the power of John's edict was limited by the fact that if the bishop's permission to go ahead with torture was not obtained within eight days, the Inquisitors could proceed on their own volition.

The official record covering Bruno's seven years in the Castel Sant'Angelo is extremely sparse, so we cannot determine unequivocally whether or not he underwent extensive torture. However, it is hard to imagine a man with Bruno's pedigree serving so long a term in the prisons of the Roman Inquisition without suffering the sadistic attentions of his jailers and persecutors. We know the evil these men perpetrated, and we know how they felt about Bruno, perhaps the most loathed heretic of his or any age.

· VIII ·

IN THE PRISONS
OF THE INQUISITION

We shall prove that they are weak, that they are mere pitiable children, but that the happiness of a child is the sweetest of all. They will grow timid and begin looking up to us and cling to us in fear, as chicks to the hen. They will marvel at us and be terrified of us and be proud that we are so mighty and so wise as to be able to tame such a turbulent flock of thousands of millions. They will be helpless and in constant fear of our wrath, their minds will grow timid, their eyes will be always shedding tears like women and children, but at the slightest sign from us they will be just as ready to pass to mirth and laughter. Oh, we shall permit them to sin, too, for they are weak and helpless, and they will love us like children for allowing them to sin.

—Fyodor Dostoyevsky,
"The Grand Inquisitor," *The Brothers Karamazov*

T HE RECORDS TELL us that Bruno was "cast into the Prison of the Roman Inquisition, February 27, 1593."[1] But after that for almost six years, we know close to nothing about him. No official records of Bruno's first six years in the Rome

---

1. Doc. Rom. iii.

prison have survived. Our knowledge of this period comes only in fleeting glimpses, fragmented accounts, stray reports from visitors, and the paradigm provided by heretics past.

Various attempts have been made to explain this anomaly, but none is entirely satisfactory. It is possible Bruno was simply kept in solitary confinement for the duration and made no appearances before the Inquisition between 1593 and 1599. Another theory is that the time was spent by the Inquisition gathering information on Bruno. But even though the Church worked at exceptionally slow speed, six years is an inordinately long time for such a task; most of the man's books were relatively easy to obtain, and the Papal Office had enormous resources to draw upon. Given these circumstances it seems likely that records were kept but have simply been lost.

Clement VIII, who had ascended to the papacy in 1592, was a relatively liberal pope, while his two primary advisers, Robert Bellarmine and Santoro di Santa Severina, held hard-line views concerning infringement of doctrine. Clement had shown himself to be an outstanding diplomat. In 1595 he had overseen the Europe-wide acceptance of Henry of Navarre as the legitimate king of France while successfully appeasing Philip of Spain, who had also been a legitimate claimant to the throne. It is possible that Clement may have quietly admired both Bruno's courage and his intellect and genuinely wished to turn him back to orthodoxy.

Bellarmine, the pope's personal theologian, was the most academically accomplished man in the Vatican, a Jesuit who by the time Bruno was imprisoned had been a professor of theology almost twenty years. On all matters of doctrine, Clement turned to Bellarmine, and for his trouble the pope was offered clear and conventional wisdom. Bellarmine rejected totally every aspect of Copernican heliocentric theory and did more than anyone of his time to hold back the flood of secular intellectual progress, earning him the epithet "Hammer of the Heretics." He distrusted science and mathematics, and long after Bruno's execution he did his utmost to undermine the ideas of Galileo. During his career he placed a long and varied list of books on the *Index Librorum Prohibitorum*.

Severina was no intellectual, but he burned with a fervent loathing of heresy in all its forms. At root an imperialist, he imagined the Vatican as a superstate, glorying in earthly power as it administered the link between God and humankind. When Clement had become the preferred choice for pope in 1592, Severina was deeply embittered, as he had hoped to wear the papal miter himself. His resentment fueled further his aggressive vision of the world and the role of the Church, causing his bloodlust to become still more exaggerated.

Because we know so little of the first six years Bruno spent in the Roman prison it is not possible to say who was responsible for his day-to-day treatment. Severina's taste for pain and his desire to persecute might have meant Giordano Bruno received the cardinal's special attention, in which case he would have suffered repeated bouts of the most severe torture and almost unimaginable privation. But it is equally possible that Clement had taken a personal interest in the Nolan and succeeded in tempering Severina's ferocity.

Unfortunately, we have no eyewitness accounts of Bruno's treatment, and if any records of his torture by the Inquisition were kept, they too have disappeared. All we have to go on is the way in which contemporaries and other heretics were treated by their jailers and persecutors. Most notable is the example of Tommaso Campanella, a man often compared with Bruno, a heretic both Bellarmine and Severina knew well, for they had imprisoned him and advised his torture.

In 1591, as Bruno was about to return to Italy, Campanella, a peripatetic magus, published a philosophical tract which outraged the Holy Office and led to his incarceration in Rome, where he spent much of the next quarter century suffering repeated torture and solitary confinement. A friend who had been allowed to visit Campanella described his condition. "His legs were all bruised and his buttocks almost without flesh, which had been torn off bit by bit in order to drag out of him a confession of the crimes of which he had been accused."[2] During a period of imprisonment by the Inquisition between 1594 and 1595, Campanella was tortured a total of twelve times, the last occasion lasting a staggering forty hours. Perhaps Bruno was treated just as cruelly.

For long stretches of time Bruno would have lain in a cell that was cast in almost total darkness, rank, tomblike, deathly still, freezing in winter, an airless oven in summer.

---

2. Lynn Thorndike, *A History of Magic and Experimental Science*, vol. 7 (New York, 1958), p. 292. It is worth noting that the accuracy of this description is questionable because the description of Campanella's injuries do not tally with the Inquisition's practice of torturing victims using only methods that cause little or no bleeding.

He had plenty of time in which to think, to remember, and for Bruno, a master of the art of memory, such reflections must have been clear but painful. On the one hand, he could recall the millions of images stored in his mind, summon up details of his past and with them alleviate the physical pain and the piercing loneliness. But on the other hand, this talent must have haunted him, as such a powerful memory undoubtedly distilled dreams of freedom, offered up recollections of fresh air and sunshine, making him yearn to escape.

Bruno was a man with a powerful ego, supremely confident and possessed of an almost indestructible sense of self-worth. Yet, the solitude, the surety that he would never experience freedom again, the knowledge that execution might not be far off, must have affected him deeply. There would almost certainly have been many times when he doubted himself, doubted the value of what he had done and what he was still doing. And beyond this, even if he never lost conviction, he could not have known the true power of his resistance to the Inquisition, leaving him uncertain what possible impact his actions would have.

And what would Bruno have contemplated during less agonizing periods? Surveying the arch of his life, would he have pondered his actions and questioned the decisions he had made? And if so, what would he have concluded?

One of the pivotal moments in his life had come with the decision to follow his master plan, the dream of using the influence of an internationally powerful figurehead to help produce a dynamic change in the attitudes of the orthodox Church toward his ideas. Henry III of France, the man Bruno called "this most

Christian, holy, religious, and pure monarch," had been his first target, but he was ill-suited to the task.[3] He had then set his sights on Queen Elizabeth of England, but she too had been an inappropriate choice, for she had wanted only to play safe and to maintain the status quo; she had little appetite for further religious turmoil. To achieve her goals (aims that were altogether more orthodox than Bruno's plans), Elizabeth would only contemplate the prosaic, the tried and tested.

Thus thwarted, Bruno lost hope in this project, at least until the political situation changed again, and he turned to a new scheme. Evidence suggests that between 1589 and 1591 (the final years before his return to Italy) Bruno had tried briefly to establish his own cult. According to an anonymous witness for the Inquisition in Rome, Bruno "said that formerly the works of Luther were much prized in Germany, but that after they tasted of his [Bruno's] works they sought for no others, and that he had begun a new sect in Germany, and if he could get out of prison he would return there to organize it better and that he wished that they should call themselves *Giordanisti*. . . ."[4]

It is possible that after coming to accept that no great political or religious figure would be in a position to project his sociospiritual vision, and before placing his faith in converting the pope, Bruno may have briefly considered organizing a group or cult to act as a basis for a new religion. Perhaps for a while he saw this as the only way left to heal the rift in the religious and social

---

3. Giordano Bruno, *De gli eroici fuori* (Paris, 1585).
4. Angelo Mercati, *Il sommario del processo di Giordano Bruno* (Vatican City, 1942), p. 61.

fabric of Europe. Indeed, there is some evidence to support the theory that the mystical brotherhood known as the Rosicrucians (who published their manifesto the *Fama* in 1614) was initiated by Bruno himself.

It is certainly true that Bruno was associated with some of the most powerful and influential figures in the occult world of the 1580s, including John Dee, whom Bruno met during his stay in England. Dee and his associate Edward Kelly were known to have played a seminal role in establishing the doctrinal foundations of the Rosicrucians, and Bruno, who traveled from France to Germany in 1585, shared many of Dee's convictions and Hermetic ideas. Twenty years after Bruno's death a prominent French occultist and writer, Gabriel Naudé, wrote a widely circulated report in which he listed the names of eight philosophers whose ideas he believed lay behind the manifesto of the Rosicrucians. The list included John Dee, Raymond Lully, Paracelsus, and Giordano Bruno.[5]

The Rosicrucians were a secret society that taught an iconoclastic form of Christian Hermeticism. They were convinced of the psychologically empowering use of symbology and ritual. Many of their doctrines were retrogressive, placing as they did great emphasis upon the *prisca sapientia*. But like Bruno's philosophy, the doctrine of the Rosicrucians also spoke of unification, of using the exciting vistas offered by the new natural philosophy. It is therefore no coincidence that many names usually identified

---

5. Gabriel Naudé, *Instruction à la France sur la vérité de l'histoire des Frères de la Rose-Croix* (Paris, 1623), pp. 15–16.

with the founding of the Royal Society and the earliest gestation of the Enlightenment have also been linked with the Rosicrucians.[6]

At the time, Bruno certainly had no shortage of support from the rich and influential. There were many who would have given him the financing to start his own sect and to protect him in lands beyond the reach of the Inquisition. Most important of these was a highly respected intellectual and occultist named John Wechel, who arranged accommodation at a Carmelite monastery in Frankfurt for Bruno and provided him with a means of support.[7] But even though Bruno had the opportunity to create and lead a potentially powerful sect, he turned away from this path and chose instead to concoct a new and altogether more radical and dangerous scheme. Little more than a year after arriving in Frankfurt, he was once more packing his few belongings and organizing plans for another journey, one that would lead to the court of the Venetian Inquisition.

When first considering what Bruno told the Venetian Inquisition, we are left confused. He contradicts himself, tells obvious

---

6. See Frances A. Yates, *The Rosicrucian Enlightenment* (London, 1972).

7. It would seem that even before he arrived in Frankfurt during the summer of 1590, information that Bruno was moving into more radical territory had extended beyond the circle of magi and Hermeticists who shared Bruno's ideals. When Bruno applied for permission to live with Wechel (a process comparable to applying for a visa), the usually liberal-minded administrators of Frankfurt made it clear they did not approve of him. A note in the *Burgomaster Reports* dated July 2, 1590, tells us, "It has been resolved that his [Bruno's] petition [to take up residence with Wechel] be refused and that he be told to take his penny elsewhere." *Burgomaster Reports*, Frankfurt, no. 160, p. 48, Frankfurt City Records Office. Presumably, the Carmelite monastery lay beyond the jurisdiction of the burgomaster.

lies (such as his declarations concerning his involvement with the occult tradition), and alternates between pious recanting and defiance. It is tempting to believe Bruno was insane, but this is difficult to justify when we consider the clarity with which he delivers his arguments and that only days before his arrest he was holding forth in philosophical discourse with Venetian intellectuals.

Instead, it would appear that from his arrival in Venice to his expulsion from the city some eighteen months later, Bruno had contrived every move and manipulated those around him with consummate skill. From Frankfurt, Bruno had kept Mocenigo waiting, played with him, pushed him to the edge. The months Bruno had spent in Padua had been another contrivance, a move to further frustrate his noble patron. Of course, Bruno knew well how the Inquisitors worked: they had been his lifelong enemies. He knew they wanted him placed before an official court and tried according to the rule book; and through his contacts in Venice (especially Ciotto, to whom Mocenigo had spoken candidly of his guest), Bruno must have known precisely what Mocenigo was planning and to whom he was answerable.

Rather than being the testimony of a madman, it is clear that Bruno's performance before the court had been a flawless masterpiece of manipulation and deception. Bruno was obsessed with the occult world of pure spirit, but he had survived a peripatetic career filled with danger and had always stayed one step ahead of his enemies. To keep alive and to keep finding support, he had to be worldly-wise and politically astute. So, considering Bruno's character and strength of conviction, his disappointment over his failure to use a statesman as a figurehead for his scheme, and the evidence of his performance in the Venetian court, it becomes clear that before his return to Italy Bruno had calculated carefully the moves he was to make if he was to fulfill his ultimate ambitions.

Bruno anticipated the political difficulties his case would cause the Venetians. He understood the delicate relationship between Venice and Rome, and he also knew that the Venetian Inquisition was far more liberal than its Roman counterpart. Nevertheless, he did not underestimate the danger and was extremely careful about what he said during the trial. Only in this way could he assure himself that in Venice there was only a very slim chance of facing execution as a heretic.

So Bruno calculated that this dangerous game had two possible outcomes. If he was extremely fortunate, the Venetians would free him and he might have a chance to remain unmolested in Venice and to teach there. If, however, the Venetians succumbed to pressure from Rome, he would be extradited and this would give him the chance to make direct contact with the pope. Once in the same room as Clement, Bruno believed he could fulfill his mission to convert the Holy Father himself and to lead the world to a new dawn.

To us, this may seem like a crazy notion, but Bruno was not only energized by his own determination, self-confidence, and sense of mission, he believed a confluence of factors would aid him significantly. In 1591, Henry of Navarre had overwhelmed the armies of the Catholic League (an extremist group financed by the Spanish monarchy) and had begun a campaign that would (by 1598) gain him the French crown. To Bruno and many other radicals throughout Europe, this grand success signaled the possibility that Rome would be forced toward a path of moderation, herald-ing a new age of religious tolerance and liberal Catholicism.

Bruno learned of this turn of events while in Frankfurt, at the very same time Mocenigo's letters of invitation were growing more insistent, and it offered him valuable encouragement. But later, soon after Bruno's arrival in Venice and as he proceeded with his design, he was given another boost when he heard stunning news from Rome concerning the occultist Francesco Patrizi.

In 1591, Patrizi published a work entitled *Nova de universis philosophia*, which detailed his own "new philosophy," a liberal Catholicism which was certainly heterodox but admittedly less radical than Bruno's own. In his treatise Patrizi called for the Church to seek better ways to treat heretics and proposed that instead of using "ecclesiastical censures or force of arms," a blend of the Hermetic tradition and Christian theology would lead many more people to religious devotion and piety.[8] He then took the bold step of dedicating his book to Pope Gregory XIV.

Within months of its publication, Pope Gregory died sud-denly and Clement VIII took the throne in Rome. Learning of *Nova de universis philosophia*, the new pope immediately summoned Patrizi to the Vatican. Occultists across Europe were amazed when the philosopher set off obediently for Rome and quickly con-cluded that he would probably disappear into the dungeons of the Inquisition. But no harm came to Patrizi; instead of facing charges of heresy he was rewarded by Clement with a chair at the University of Rome.

---

8. Luigi Firpo, *Gli scritti di Francesco Pucci* (Turin, 1957), pp. 182–83.

So Bruno had some right to feel he too could influence the pope and change the structure of Catholicism. But in reaching this conclusion he had made three serious errors. First, the impact of Henry of Navarre's conquest of France would only defuse religious tension in Europe after many more years of struggle, and this change would come far too late to influence Bruno's plans. Second, Bruno had placed too much importance upon Patrizi's reception in Rome. Patrizi was a philosopher whose theological arguments were altogether less radical than Bruno's. But, crucially, unlike Bruno, Patrizi was flexible; he was a man who was able to compromise. Indeed, soon after starting his course at the university, Patrizi had inflamed the sensibilities of the Inquisition but kept his chair by obediently toning down the content of his lectures.

Bruno's third error was to overestimate the power of the pope. Clement was an intellectual and a relatively liberal pontiff, but like most popes, he did not control the machinations of the Vatican alone. He had powerful enemies, and he relied upon his advisers, who were for the most part more hard-line than he, particularly in the matter of heresy and the treatment of radical thinkers.

Bruno's scheme had taken him to the Inquisitors' prisons, so close to the Holy Office, yet once there he was utterly powerless.

The earliest record of any form of trial of Bruno in Rome is dated January 14, 1599, a little less than five years and eleven months after Bruno's imprisonment in the city. A congregation consisting of eight cardinals, seven coadjutors, and an official notary was present.

Two of the leading members of the congregation were Severina and Bellarmine (who would be made a cardinal later that year). The records report that Bruno's books had been studied along with the records of his Venetian trial, from which a long list of pernicious heresies had been produced. These were read before the congregation, eight of the most heinous were selected, and a note was made that the papers and manuscripts would be subjected to further study in search of still deeper aberrations.

Sadly, the record does not itemize the eight chosen heresies, and these were not quoted in subsequent hearings. Bruno continued to deny that he had in any way acted as a heretic or written heretical material.

In most trials of heretics, this denial would offer clues about the nature of the charges, but not so with the Nolan. Many heretics accepted the label, but Bruno's view of heresy was very different from that of his persecutors. He held core religious beliefs (the existence of God, the importance of Christ, the sanctity of communion); his support of these was unshakable, and we have to accept that he did not speak against them to others. But Bruno's religious understanding was far broader than that of the cardinals devoted to orthodoxy. To Bellarmine, to Severina, and to the other judges arrayed against Bruno, the notion that life might exist beyond the earth, the idea that God could not have created merely a single home for life, that all things were interconnected on some nebulous spiritual plane, that the Holy Trinity was merely a confusion of words, all this would have resounded with the deepest tones of the heretic, outrages to be purged only by the cleansing power of the flame. Bruno saw none of this as heretical, and in his own inimitable style he could find ways to successfully coalesce his thoughts and views with the elements of orthodoxy he purported to honor.

At a second congregation three weeks later, six cardinals, seven coadjutors, and a notary gathered and Bruno was called upon to answer the charges of heresy. The report tells us that the accused argued against each of the eight points, but it does not tell us what he said. Indeed, aside from the description of the hearing made by the notary, the only other morsel to survive is a note in the archive written in a different hand from the notary's that tells us: "His Holiness decrees and ordains that it be intimated to him by the Father in Theology, Bellarmine and the Commissary that all these propositions are heretical, and not now declared so for the first time, but by the most ancient Fathers of the Church and the Apostolic Chair. If we shall acknowledge this, good; if less, a term of forty days shall be allowed."[9]

This statement is a clear indication of the conflict that had been playing out during the six years of Bruno's imprisonment in Rome. It demonstrates both a severe tone, reiterating the charges of heresy, and a remarkable degree of tolerance in that Bruno is here offered another forty days in which to recant.

But forty days turned into nine months and more. What passed between the prisoner and the accusers is again unknown. It is most likely that Bruno argued his case with such skill that the learned judges were unsure how to deal with him within the limits of Church law. If nothing else, the extended period of grace

---

9. Doc. Rom. xviii.

Bruno was given demonstrates how his accusers were confused, lacking unity over the details of their claims and torn by conflicting emotions the man fostered in them. Based on what we know of Bellarmine, he would have argued that the heretic was entirely wrong, his statements worthless imaginings. But he needed Bruno to admit to this, to take back his claims and to confirm their falsity. Bellarmine could not yet face the prospect of simply having Bruno dragged to the stake without a recantation. Severina, a man from a very different mold, a man who cared nothing for intellectual games, would have tried his utmost to persuade the pope to burn Bruno as quickly as possible. In Severina's eyes, this particularly repulsive little heretic was not merely a thorn in the side of the Holy See but a tangible threat to the stability of the Church. And yet, these men could not sign Bruno's death warrant. As much as they could manipulate and coerce, they needed Clement's support, and his remained the voice of tolerance. But there were limits even to his famed patience.

The *Sacro Arsenale*, the Inquisitors' "handbook," informs us: "If the culprit denies the indictments and these be not fully proved and he, during the term assigned to him to prepare his defense, have not cleared himself from the imputations which result from the process, it is necessary to have the truth out of him by a rigorous examination." In other words, the heretic is given a period of time in which to recant, and if he does not confess then, he must be tortured until a statement is wrenched from him.

It is almost certain that Bruno faced torture during this period of his imprisonment, torture both officially sanctioned by Clement and conducted by stealth beyond the papal gaze. It was during the same stage of the process of persecution against Tommaso Campanella that he was so ruthlessly mutilated in an attempt to make him denounce his humanistic views, and there can be little doubt fire, water, steel, and rope were employed in an effort to make Bruno reposition the sun in orbit about the earth and to vanquish the specter of nonhuman beings breathing God's alien air.

Again, there are no reports, no eyewitness accounts, to describe Bruno's burns or torn ligaments, but the trace of the Inquisitor's fingers and the wickedness that lit up the darkened cell with the torturer's fire are there in the sense of irresistible stubbornness and resolve Bruno displayed during his final months. For torture merely hardened Bruno's feelings. Rather than collapsing before the horrors inflicted upon him, Bruno struck back by utterly refusing to give way and by his growing commitment to martyrdom. As the days ebbed away, as he argued over every point of doctrine held against him, and as he saw his dream of direct personal contact with His Holiness dissolve to nothing, he knew the belief that had sustained him was untenable and a new role awaited him.

On December 21, 1599, Bruno was brought before the Inquisition again. This time, nine cardinals, including Bellarmine and Severina, faced him. Bruno again argued his case, addressing the eight points of heresy. "He was heard," runs the report, ". . . concerning all his pretensions." When asked if he would now recant, he said: "I will not do so. I have nothing to renounce, neither do I know what I should renounce." Gone was Bruno the actor. Gone the Bruno who had orchestrated his own arrest and had played the Venetian Inquisition as a virtuoso bows Stradivarius strings. Here was a man calcified by pain, rigid with determination and self-absorption.

Yet, amazingly, the cardinals still held back; again, Clement tempered their rage. Bruno infuriated each of them, but equally they were all, in their own ways, determined to break him. He had shown himself to be unbending; physical agony merely strengthened his resolve. They would try another approach.

"It is thus decided," a surviving fragment of a report informs us, ". . . his blind and false doctrine should be made manifest to him, and Hippolytus Maria and Paulus della Mirandola be appointed to deal with the said brother and point out to him the propositions to be abjured, so that he may recognize his errors and amend and recant; and show him all the good they can as soon as possible."[10]

And so, over the festive season and into the new century, the two academics appointed by the court attended Bruno. They sat in his cell day after day and argued through the finer points of his ideas and his heretical doctrine as it had been laid out in his many books and lectures. The academics, the general of the Dominican Order, the Reverend Father Hippolytus Maria Beccaria, and the procurator of the order, Father Paulus della Mirandola, were Bellarmine's acolytes. A figure so grand as the newly appointed cardinal would not stoop to visit Bruno in person, but

---

10. Doc. Rom. xxiv2 and xxiv3.

his representatives served their master faithfully in the task of trying to turn Bruno from his own convictions, divert him from the path he had etched for himself.

Clement too needed to make some form of contact with this man whom none could break. He sent his personal confessor, Cardinal Cesare Baronius, to talk to the heretic. Baronius, an intellectual who was then midway through his twelve-volume masterpiece of Counter Reformation propaganda, *Annales ecclesiastici,* and who gave the pope daily absolution at confessional, reported to Clement on every detail of his conversations with Bruno.[11] But clearly, Baronius never succeeded in gaining Bruno's trust, because if he had, this would have provided the personal link with Clement that Bruno craved. The fact that nothing came of their conversations strongly suggests Bruno and Cardinal Baronius had not established any form of understanding. Furthermore, Baronius failed utterly to alter Bruno's views. And Bellarmine's stooges, Hippolytus Beccaria and Paulus della Mirandola, were equally unsuccessful in their quest.

On January 20, 1600, Bruno appeared before the congregation again. Once again, Severina, Bellarmine, and seven other cardinals were arrayed before the prisoner. Bruno was asked once more if he was willing to recant. He refused utterly, knowing that the time had long since passed when anything but death at the stake awaited him. If he recanted, he would be burned; if he did not, he would be burned. He was beyond all help.

---

11. Domenico Berti, *Vita di Giordano Bruno da Nola* (Turin, 1868), Appendix I.

Nineteen days later, he was brought before the cardinals once more and asked one final time if he was willing to recant. He was not. And so the long cruel indictment was read aloud: "On the 4th February 1599, a year ago, it was determined that the eight heretical propositions should once more be presented to thee, and this was done on the 15th, that shouldst thou recognize them as heretical and abjure them, then thou wouldst be received for penitence; but, if not, then shouldst thou be condemned on the fortieth day from then for repentance; and thou didst declare thyself ready to recognize these eight propositions as heretical and detest and abjure them in such place and time as might please the Holy Office, and not only these propositions, but thou didst declare thyself ready to make thine obedience concerning the others which were shown to thee. But then, since thou didst present further writings to the Holy Office addressed to His Holiness and to Us, whereby it was manifest that thou didst pertinaciously adhere to thine aforesaid errors; and information having been received that at the Holy Office of Vercelli thou hadst been denounced because in England thou wast esteemed an atheist and didst compose a work about a Triumphant Beast, therefore on the 10th September 1599, thou wast given forty days in which to repent, and it was determined that at the end of these days proceedings should be taken against thee as is ordained and commanded by the Holy Canon Law; and since thou didst nevertheless remain obstinate and impertinent in thine aforesaid errors and heresies, there were sent unto thee the Reverend Father Hippolytus Maria Beccaria and Father Paul Isario della Mirandola that they might admonish and persuade thee to recognize thy most grave errors and heresies. But thou has ever persisted with obstinate pertinacity in these thine erroneous and heretical opinions. Wherefore the accusation brought against thee has been examined and considered with the confession of thy pertinacious and obstinate errors and heresies, even while thy didst deny them to be such, and all else was observed and considered; thy case was brought before our general Congregation held in the presence of His Holiness on 20th January last and after voting and resolution we decided on the following sentence.

"Having invoked the name of Our Lord Jesus Christ and of his most Glorious Mother Mary ever Virgin in the cause and aforesaid causes brought before the Holy Office between on the one hand, the Reverend Giulio Monterenzi, Doctor of Laws, Procurator Fiscal of the said Holy Office, and on the other, thyself, the aforesaid, Giordano Bruno, the accused, examined, brought to trial and found guilty, impertinent, obstinate, and pertinacious; in this our final sentence determined by the counsel and opinion of our advisers the Reverend Fathers, Masters in Sacred Theology and Doctors in both Laws, our advisers: We hereby, in these documents, publish, announce, pronounce, sentence, and declare thee, the aforesaid Brother Giordano Bruno, to be an impenitent and pertinacious heretic, and therefore to have incurred all the ecclesiastical censures and pains of the Holy Canon, the Laws and the Constitutions, both general and particular, imposed on such confessed impenitent, pertinacious, and obstinate heretics. Wherefore as such we verbally degrade thee and declare thou must be degraded, and we hereby ordain and command that thou shalt be actually degraded for all thine ecclesiastical orders both major and minor in which thou has been ordained, according to the Sacred Canon Law: and that thou must be driven forth, and we do drive thee forth from our ecclesiastical forum and from our holy and immaculate Church of whose mercy thou art become unworthy. Furthermore, we condemn, we reprobate, and we prohibit all thine aforesaid and thy other books and writings as heretical and erroneous, containing many heresies and errors, and we ordain that all of them which have come or may in future come into the hands of the Holy Office shall be publicly destroyed and burned in the square of St. Peter before the steps and that they shall be placed upon the Index of Forbidden Books, and as we have commanded, so shall be done."[12]

And this is where our story began, before this congregation of February 8. On that occasion, Bruno's personal letter to the pope was opened but not shown to the pontiff. But of course, by now this hardly mattered anyway; the time had passed when anything could sway the thinking of Bruno's judges. They could not now be swayed by anything. As the world had shuffled into a new century, nervous voices were raised in the Vatican. News of fanatical cults that believed in heralding an anti-Catholic age that could destabilize Europe put new fear into the minds of the cardinals. And

12. Doc. Rom. xxvi.

because of this, Bruno's execution had now become an imperative. And another factor in pushing the Inquisition to act came from the Spanish, close allies of the Vatican.

A few months before Bruno's final hearing, the Spanish Inquisition, a body that acted quite independently of its Roman counterpart, had put down a religious uprising of discontented Dominicans led by the religious radical Tommaso Campanella. Campanella had inflamed a small band of heretical Dominicans to protest against their order and to proselytize the idea that the year 1600 would mark a global revolution in the Church and reshape Catholicism. This uprising was known as the Calabrian Revolt, because it had begun in Calabria (now part of southern Italy), an area then under Spanish control. The Spanish were therefore even more concerned over the arrival of the new century than was the Papal Office and considered Bruno a threat. When, early in 1600, an adulterous couple from the papal court had eloped to Spanish territory and were apprehended, an exchange of favors was quickly agreed. The couple would be extradited to Rome to face trial if Bruno was burned.

But the Holy Office had already decided Bruno's fate; the only question was when the sentence should be carried out. To appease their Spanish neighbors, the Inquisitors may have brought the execution forward, but even that is uncertain. By this time, Clement had lost any remaining scrap of patience for the bedraggled little man before him and he would no longer stand in the way of his cardinals. Bellarmine had resigned himself to a Pyrrhic victory; he could not make Bruno recant. And so a final scene would be played out during which another dissenter would be sacrificed at the altar of dogma, another would join the hundreds of thousands slaughtered in the name of orthodoxy.

Led from the congregation and later that day handed over to the secular arm, Bruno was taken away to prepare himself for the waiting flames.

· IX ·

THE CURTAIN FALLS

Oh difficulties to be endured, cries the coward, the feather-head, the shuttlecock, the faint-heart. The task is not impossible, though hard. The craven must stand aside. Ordinary, easy tasks are for the commonplace and the herd. Rare, heroic, and divine men overcome the difficulties of the way and force an immortal palm from necessity. You may fail to reach your goal, but run the race nevertheless. Put forth your strength in so high a business. Strive on with your last breath.

—Giordano Bruno

O N THE MORNING of his execution, Giordano Bruno was visited by members of the Brotherhood of Pity of St. John the Beheaded, a group who ministered to any heretic they could in an effort to do what the Inquisition had failed to do, to lead them meekly back to the one true faith. From the records of the brotherhood we learn: "At the second hour of the night, information came that Justice would be done on an impenitent friar in the morning. Hence, at the sixth hour of the night, the Comforters and the chaplain assembled at S. Ursula and went to the prison in the Tower of Nona, entered the chapel, and offered up the winter prayers. To them was consigned the man, Giordano Bruno, son of Gioan Bruno, an apostate friar of Nola in the Kingdom, an impenitent. He was exhorted by our brothers in all love, and two Fathers of the Order of St. Dominic, two of the Order of Jesus, two of the new church and one of St. Jerome were called in. These with all loving zeal and much learning, showed him his error, yet he stood firm throughout and to the end in his accursed obstinacy, setting his brain and mind to a thousand errors and vain-gloryings."[1]

What must Bruno have thought during those final hours? Did he despair, finally? Did he reach the conclusion he had been wrong all along? Or did he feel vindicated, confident that his thoughts would survive the flames? Did he perhaps wonder if far away, on the alien worlds he imagined, other creatures burned their dreamers too?

At 5:30 A.M. on February 19, a Thursday and a feast day in Rome, Bruno was led in chains from San Ursula. He was dressed in a white ankle-length robe illuminated with the cross of St. Andrew and dotted with painted devils holding their long, barbed tails against a backdrop of crudely daubed crimson flames. The route was crowded with the virtuous and the curious. Much had been made of this burning. A primitive form of newsletter, *Avvisi e ricordi*, had even been printed to inform people of the occasion: "An entertaining judicial burning was expected," it declared. According to this tabloid of the day, "Bruno has declared he will die a willing martyr and that his soul will rise with the smoke to

---

1. Doc. Rom. xxix.

paradise."[2] Copies of the newsletter had been passed throughout the excited crowd and trampled upon along the wet road. As the parade moved on, Bruno became animated and excited. He reacted to the mocking crowds, responding to their yells with quotes from his books and the sayings of the ancients. His comforters, the Brotherhood of St. John, tried to quiet the exchange, to protect Bruno from yet further pain and indignity, but he ignored them. And so after a few minutes the procession was halted by the Servants of Justice. A jailer was brought forward and another two held Bruno's head rigid. A long metal spike was thrust through Bruno's left cheek, pinning his tongue and emerging through the right cheek. Then another spike was rammed vertically through his lips. Together, the spikes formed a cross. Great sprays of blood erupted onto his gown and splashed the faces of the brotherhood close by. Bruno spoke no more.

A few minutes later the procession arrived at the site of execution, the Campo di Fiori, the Field of Flowers, where, in one corner, opposite the Theater of Pompeii, the stake had been prepared. The guards led Bruno to the thick wooden post, shoved him up against it, and wrapped a thick rope around him, across his shoulders, his chest, his waist, and his legs. The faggots (about which Bruno had once joked) were piled up to the condemned man's chin and the torch placed between his feet. The flames caught quickly in the light morning breeze.

It has been claimed that many victims of the stake were saved a

---

2. MS. Urbane 1068 (Doc. Rom. xxviii, xxxi, and xxxii), Vatican Library.

slow death by arranging a payment to the executioner who would surreptitiously snap their necks as they were tied to the post.[3] We know this did not happen to Bruno, for as the fire began to grip, the Brothers of Pity of St. John the Beheaded tried one last time to save the man's soul. Risking the flames, one of them leaned into the fire with a crucifix, but Bruno merely turned his head away. Seconds later, the fire caught his robe and seared his body, and above the hissing and crackling of the flames could be heard the man's muffled agony.

After the fire had subsided, what remained of Bruno's body was smashed to powder with hammers and the ashes were cast to the wind so that no one could save anything of the heretic as a relic. As far as the Inquisition was concerned, it had obliterated Bruno, destroyed his body, banished his memory, his ideas, his writings, his very thought, and he had been consigned to Hell.

The pope saw nothing Bruno wrote in prison, and the two men never met in private as Bruno had hoped. As Giordano burned that festive Thursday, February 19, 1600, the crowd cheered and waved their banners, children ran as close to the flames as they dared, and frightened mothers pulled them back. And when the

---

3. Other tales report that particularly reviled heretics were burned using very dry wood. This produced little smoke and so the victim would be less likely to suffocate. Instead, the flames burned and the wounds cauterized until the fire overwhelmed the victim and he died of shock. We do not know whether this worst of fates befell Bruno, but the powerful men who sanctioned his murder considered him the most extreme heretic in the history of the Church, and so it is a strong possibility.

spectacle was over and the world cleansed of another heretic, Bruno's ashes settled on ledges and in nearby fields. There the rain carried into the soil molecules that had once composed parts of his body. Over time, the molecules were broken open, their atoms absorbed by plants. The plants were eaten by animals and some found their way to the tables of Rome and beyond. Other elements of Bruno fell into water and were recycled to splash upon the faces of bathers and into drinking goblets. And so, perhaps, on an atomic level at least, the pope himself was conjoined with the heretic after all.

As Bruno would have it, the universe is infinite, and as one. We are all one another. Everything is everything else.

· X ·

ENCORE!

I wish the world to possess the glorious fruits of my labor,
to awaken the soul and open the understanding of those
who are deprived of that light which, most assuredly, is
not mine own invention. Should I be in error, I do not
believe I willfully go wrong. And in speaking and writing
as I do I am not contending through the desire of being
victorious; for I deem every kind of renown and conquest
God's foe, vile and without a particle of honor in it, if it
be not the truth; but for love of true wisdom and in the
effort to reflect aright, I weary, I rack, I torment myself.

—Giordano Bruno

O F COURSE, THIS was not the end; how could it be?
Indeed, some may see it merely as a beginning, others as a
continuation. Bruno would certainly have thought as much; a
burning that led to new life, new awakenings. The agony passed.
And, as his life ebbed away, others elsewhere began, and as Bruno's
brain fried in the flames, the thoughts and ideas that had sprung
from it survived and flourished anew.

Exactly four hundred years after Bruno's execution, enthusiasts
marked the day with tributes at the site of his burning, dedica-
tions appeared on the Web, and a stream of articles about the man

and his ideas made a prominent mark in daily newspapers far, far from the Field of Flowers. One report read: "Rome: They laid wreaths, heaped roses and, in the sincerest tribute of all, they argued, interrupted and expounded—pilgrims of free thought, paying homage yesterday at the spot where the Inquisition burned an outspoken philosopher-priest four centuries ago. A cardboard sign at the base of Bruno's statue denounced the 'infamous homicide' as if it were yesterday. A member of Italy's Radical Party, Eleanora Caparrotti, declared: 'They pardoned Galileo. But we're still waiting on Bruno.' A Vatican representative referred to the incident as a 'sad episode' and 'a matter of deep regret.'"[1]

Four hundred years after his death, Bruno has become one of those almost legendary figures who has been appropriated by all shades of the political spectrum and by a plethora of groups whose interests range from the purely philosophical to religious extremes. On the Web you may find a ten-page article about Bruno at the World Socialist website. Groups linked with NASA have gone to the trouble of writing pieces that disparage the ideas of Bruno and attempt to deflate the myth that has grown up around him. Meanwhile, the Catholic Encyclopedia entry "Giordano Bruno" at http://www.newadvent.org mysteriously makes no mention of Bruno's execution at all and goes shamelessly to great lengths to diminish both the merits of Bruno's character and the value of his work. It refers to Bruno's opinions as "errors."

---

1. Ellen Knickmeyer, "Tributes made to the martyr of free thought Giordano Bruno," Associated Press, Friday, February 18, 2000.

It may come as little surprise that the official position of the Church has remained unchanged since 1600. Indeed, almost no comment on the subject has emerged from the Vatican during the course of four centuries. Any form of official Church statement about Bruno is rare. In 1889, a group of supporters had constructed in the Field of Flowers a self-funded bronze statue cast by Ettori Ferrari in tribute to Bruno, and the move was unceremoniously condemned by the then pope, Leo XIII.[2] As recently as 1942, Cardinal Mercati, the man who discovered the lost documents relating to Bruno's Roman trial, declared that the Church had been perfectly right to burn Bruno because he had deserved it.

But of course, such statements do nothing but confirm the impact Bruno and some of his more adventurous contemporaries made. "Free philosophical speculation in Italy," the renowned scholar Luigi Firpo has pointed out, "fought its decisive battle during the pontificate of Clement VIII, in the last decade of the century. It suffered the condemnation of Telesio's *De rerum natura*, and of all the works of Bruno and Campanella. It was crippled by the investigations opened against Giambattista della Porta, Col'Antonio Stigiola, and Cesare Cremonini, by the beginning of Campanella's long imprisonment, by the execution of Francesco Pucci, and by the burning of Bruno."[3] Naturally, the losses and the suffering of the martyrs to free thought and the freedom of

---

2. The renowned evolutionary biologist and friend of Darwin Ernst Haeckel composed an address for this event.

3. Luigi Firpo, "Il processo di Giordano Bruno" (Rome, 1993), p. 145.

the intellect could not last forever; battles were lost, but the war could go only one way.

In order to appraise what Bruno's efforts have meant for the generations that followed him, we need, at least initially, to deconstruct his vision and trace the way his ideas have filtered into the work of a range of individuals and helped to shape whole disciplines, some of which have begun to emerge only in recent years. Bruno was a man of so many parts and amalgamated so much that it is inevitable he would inspire a variety of thinkers who followed him.

The period immediately after Bruno's arrest in Venice was, of course, a dangerous time for his friends and associates, but there were no further arrests or persecutions among those with whom he had associated. Bruno's assistant Besler vanished, and he appears to have wisely disassociated himself from Bruno's legacy to the point where nothing is known of his fate. However, copies in Besler's hand constitute the only original surviving versions of some of Bruno's works. Manuscripts of nine treatises transcribed by Besler, now known as the Noroff Manuscripts, are currently in the Moscow Library, along with an original copy of Bruno's *De magia* (*On Magic*), which the author dedicated to his amanuensis. Other philosophers and occultists Bruno had met in Germany did maintain an interest in Brunian philosophy outside Italy. Most significant was a young student of Bruno's named Raffaele Eglin, who in 1595 published a collection of his master's lectures even as their creator suffered the agonies of the Inquisition dungeons in Rome. However, much of the work of these early disciples fell into obscurity, and for many years most of Bruno's teachings were forgotten. Yet his legacy survived, thanks to the impact of his ideas upon the work of a varied group of influential thinkers.

First we should consider the scientific element of Bruno's work. Ironically, perhaps, this presents us with the most lateral links between his ideas and modern thinking. Bruno was not a scientist in the modern sense. For a long time, indeed for centuries, his conceptualization of natural philosophy was quite out of step with the New Science (as it became known after Galileo) and its blossoming forth into the Enlightenment and beyond.

Beyond this, Bruno was never in any sense a practical researcher. He did not think in terms of experiment or mathematics. In fact, he actively disapproved of the way the new science of his time was becoming increasingly entwined with mathematical proof and purity; Copernicus, he claimed, was "too much a mathematician and not enough a natural philosopher."[4]

And from this stance we may start to understand the true essence of Bruno's "science."

Galileo was a younger contemporary of Bruno's. He was thirty-six when Bruno was burned, and the older man's martyrdom affected him enormously. Galileo worshiped Bruno, not for his scientific methods, but for his power, the power that had come

---

4. Bruno was an "ideas man" but he had a profound effect upon many of those of his own and later generations who were interested in experiment. The best example of this is found in the work of Bruno's English contemporary William Gilbert, who met Bruno during the Nolan's stay in England during the early 1580s. In his *De magnete*, published in the year of Bruno's death, Gilbert applied thinking similar to Bruno's "universal Copernicanism" as expressed in *The Ash Wednesday Supper*, written in 1584 in London.

from his sacrifice and the power of his convictions, the power of his vision and the power of his forward-thinking. Although thousands died at the stake as martyrs, Giordano Bruno was unique. Most martyrs were people of courage and conviction, but many were insane, consumed by an inner fire. Almost all of them went to the stake for their personal vision of God, obsessing over some nuance of doctrine. Others died because they happened to be in the wrong place at the wrong time. Bruno was different because he held a broader vision; his heresy was all-embracing. He defended the right of all humans to think as they wished; he offered an alternative to the ideas enforced by orthodoxy. He was a man who wished to steer humanity toward reason, who wanted to allow us to conceptualize freely rather than have our thoughts determined for us.

Galileo, although also a natural philosopher, took a different tack from Bruno's. He pioneered the use of experiment and mathematics as a primary tool of science, and it was his ideas that led directly to the work of Isaac Newton, the Enlightenment, and the Industrial Revolution. It was his advances that gestated technology and what we now call "classical science." Bruno thought in terms of images rather than mathematics, logic and pure reasoning rather than experiment.

Many commentators from Bruno's time to the present day have viewed Bruno's philosophy as antiquated, his ideas rooted in the ancient mystical tradition alone—in short, they refer to his work disapprovingly as "pseudoscience." Some even suggest he was hypocritical to criticize Aristotle when he too applied deductive reasoning and did not back up his ideas with experiment or mathematics. But Bruno's vision was far broader than these critics allow. He was indeed retrospective in the way he utilized aspects of the occult, but he also looked forward to a pure science of clinical reasoning, albeit nonmathematical in his definition. Most important to us today, these two seemingly irreconcilable visions, the mathematical and the intuitive, are once again seen as possible partners in the search for unification. The weirdness of quantum mechanics and the possibilities of uniting it with relativity has reawakened the concept of unifying diverse disciplines. Today, there is a belief that a unity of knowledge may be found, that thinkers might not necessarily rely solely upon empirical wisdom supported by mathematics. There is a growing interest in the intuitive approach, pictorial representation, and other forms of nonmathematical expression in science.

Galileo became a professor at the University of Padua just at the time Bruno arrived in Venice, and in 1592, as Bruno faced the Venetian Inquisitors, Galileo was teaching and researching only twenty-five miles from the Venetian court. Padua was a tiny city and the university a close-knit community. It is almost unthinkable that Galileo and Bruno did not meet when Bruno taught there in early 1592, and the two men may well have exchanged ideas. Indeed, recent scholarship has pointed to clear similarities between Bruno's and Galileo's statements concerning the heliocentric model, the very matter that later led to Galileo's arrest and trial. In his *Eight Philosophers of the Italian Renaissance*, Professor P. O. Kristeller goes as far as to say, "Galileo could have read Bruno long before the latter was condemned, and the resemblance between certain passages in Galileo and Bruno that deal with the place of the earth in the universe is so great that it may not be incidental after all."[5]

However, as much as Galileo and Bruno agreed over the basic interpretation of Copernicus's great work, they held quite different views on the matter of an infinite universe. The notion of infinity lay at the core of Bruno's cosmological and teleological vision, but Galileo believed any contemplation of infinity to be a wasted effort and once declared to a friend: "Reason and my mental powers do not enable me to conceive of either finitude or infinitude." In this sense at least, Bruno's interpretation of the universe was more profound than that of Galileo.

But beyond this, a more important link between Bruno and Galileo was simply the impact Bruno's fate had upon Galileo's career and personal life. With his martyrdom, Bruno had become the model for the heretic-philosopher, and within a few years of his murder some commentators were making unwelcome comparisons between Bruno's writings and some of the more daring contributions of Galileo. One, Martin Hasdale of the court of Emperor Rudolf of Germany and a friend of Galileo's, even wrote to chastise him for not giving Bruno sufficient credit. In the letter he points out what he considered obvious similarities between comments in Galileo's *Sidereus nuncius* (*The Starry Messenger*), published in 1610, and Bruno's heliocentric vision. "I had this morning occasion for friendly dispute with Kepler," Hasdale writes, "when we were both lunching with the Ambassador to

---

5. P. O. Kristeller, *Eight Philosophers of the Italian Renaissance* (Stanford, Calif., 1964).

Saxony. . . . He said concerning your book [*Sidereus nuncius*] that truly it revealed the divinity of your talent, but that you had given cause of complaint not only to the German nation but also to your own, since you make no mention of those writers who gave the signal and the occasion for your discovery, naming among them Giordano Bruno as an Italian, Copernicus, and himself."[6]

To be fair to Galileo, although Bruno and others pointed the way to the ideas contained in *Sidereus nuncius*, unlike Galileo, these thinkers offered no form of mathematical treatment or experimental support for their ideas. Furthermore, it is understandable that Galileo would want to divorce his name from the Nolan's and to put as much distance between them publicly as possible. First, Galileo did not much care for Bruno's penchant for blending the Hermetic tradition with the new vision of natural philosophy. Galileo, perhaps the first great empiricist, favored the unceremonious dumping of "old" knowledge, subjective understanding, and the ancient Hermetic arts. He became the great standard-bearer of the new rationalism. For Galileo, mathematics was the ultimate expression of God, just as it had been for Plato. But, unlike Plato, Galileo studiously rejected mysticism.

Beyond this, Galileo had another simple and quite obvious reason for wishing to disassociate his name from Bruno's. Aware of the Nolan's left-of-center philosophies and his clearly heretical interpretations of Copernicus, Galileo would have viewed Bruno as a very dangerous man. Understandably, he would not want the

---

6. Letter dated April 15, 1610, published in E. Favaro, ed., *Galileo Galilei* (Florence, 1890–1909).

whiff of heresy hanging around him, as it had clung to Bruno. This is supported by the comments of a recent editor of Galileo's works who points out, ". . . Galileo dissociated himself from the current trend of pseudo-Pythagorean occult science and mystical rationalism, of which there had been an extraordinary revival in the late Renaissance, climaxed by the tragic fate of Bruno."[7]

Yet links between the two were almost unavoidable. Bruno's trial and testimony alerted the Papal Office to the threat of Copernicanism. This is evident from the fact that although Copernicus's *Revolutions* (which had so inspired both Bruno and Galileo) had been in circulation since 1543, it was only after Bruno's execution that it was placed on the *Index Librorum Prohibitorum* (in 1616). But with Bruno and Copernicus both dead, Galileo inevitably fell under suspicion. Turning their attention to his work, the Inquisition did not take long to find problems with his views, and in spite of his best efforts, Galileo's name was connected with Bruno's. Indeed, evidence shows that Galileo's own arrest and trial as a heretic in 1633 came about because some powerful individuals within the Vatican viewed him as a "resurrected Bruno" and believed he could be used to set a further example in the Church's struggle to eliminate heterodox philosophies.[8]

But ironically, Bruno and Galileo were very different enemies of the Inquisition. Certainly the views of each could spell (in the eyes of Vatican officials at least) the annihilation of orthodoxy and

7. Galileo Galilei, *Dialogue on the Two Great World Systems*, edited by G. Santillana (Chicago, 1953), p. 15n.

8. Edward A. Gosselin and Lawrence S. Lerner, "Galileo and the Long Shadow of Bruno," *Archives internationales d'histoire des sciences* 25, no. 97 (1975), pp. 223–46.

the dismantling of a faith-based universal vision. But Bruno offered a route only partly based upon science; his was a multifaceted paradigm, incorporating a strange resolution of opposites, the infinite and the finite, the macrocosmic and the microcosmic, religion and science, the occult and rational modeling, symbolism and ritual, mind and body, soul and brain. Galileo's vision was purer, yet enormously more prosaic, strict, utilitarian. Bruno offered a majestic free expression tempered with logic; Galileo laid before us the clean lines of unsullied reason, a noble world of rules, proofs, axioms, theorems, pressed steel, steam engines, transistors, and microchips. It was only natural that the world, already leaning as it was toward unblemished rationalism and growing enamored of the undeniable charms of number and experiment, should pursue Galileo's offerings and allow Bruno's memory to fade.

For the seventeenth-century world, Bruno's ideas offered nothing practical. Unlike Galileo's science, they gave no immediate material benefits. Inevitably, as the years passed and humanity reached the dawn of the Enlightenment, any competition between Galileo's science (championed by such demigods as Isaac Newton) and Bruno's vision could have only one outcome. And in many ways we should be immensely grateful for this: classical science was incredibly successful and changed our world utterly, and we continue to reap the benefits.

But the first off the block does not always win the race. Around 1910, something strange started to happen in the world of science. Suddenly, scientists who had been weaned on classical science began to delve deeper, and they revealed some uncomfortable facts. Technology that had sprung from classical science worked, of course it worked; but there was no clear explanation for why it worked. Classical scientists had been acting like those of us who use a DVD player every day but with no real understanding of how the circuitry allows televised images to be stored on a disc and played back on a TV screen.

As a consequence, in order to find accurate explanations for what they observed, classical physicists were forced to rethink and reevaluate many of their most fundamental and cherished notions. They had to reinvent the very way they thought about science. They used mathematics (it was still the best tool they had), but they also allowed themselves to think more freely, intuitively, instinctively. Most important, although few scientists of the time were familiar with Bruno's ideas, they began to incorporate some of his methods into the way they worked; in particular, they began to think in terms of images. Suddenly, the idea of "thought experiments" (a concept Bruno had made popular during the 1580s after developing his art of memory) became absolutely indispensable to the visionary quantum mechanist. Schrödinger gave us his cats, Heisenberg his uncertainty principle, concepts that threw our view of the universe into a pool of randomness and chance; each became a cornerstone of a new discipline, the panorama of quantum mechanics.[9]

---

9. In one of Bruno's thought experiments he imagined himself floating above and beyond the earth. As he drifted closer and closer to the moon he visualized it growing larger as the earth became smaller. From the surface of the moon itself, the earth seemed like a satellite and the moon had taken on the dimensions of the earth. Traveling farther still, he imagined both the earth and the moon as specks of light. Eventually they disappeared into endless night. From this he

Quantum mechanics turned classical science on its head, and the pioneers of the field (de Broglie, Dirac, Heisenberg, and Bohr) saw increasingly the huge rewards to be gained by thinking laterally and fusing pure mathematics with visual images. To a degree, scientists began to conceptualize as Bruno had done, rather than only as Galileo had taught them.

Naturally, modern science is still infused with mathematics; it is indispensable. But in recent years many theoreticians have begun to use visual images and logic pictures in their work, and have found the technique a powerful method for tackling resistant problems. The best example of this comes from the work of one of the greatest thinkers of the twentieth century, Richard Feynman, who created what have become known as Feynman diagrams, pictorial representations of complex subnuclear transactions.

And Bruno's vision of picture logic is actually used by almost everyone in the industrialized world each day, for we live in a world dominated by computers, and computers are machines that generate images. With computers using Windows software, we are all now thinking pictorially and learning to understand concepts based upon logically connected images. This is exactly what Bruno was doing over four hundred years ago when he developed ancient techniques for enhancing memory. He also employed these tools

---

determined a primitive form of nonmathematical relativity in which he emphasized the fact that the appearance and the reality of things are not always the same. To us, the vision of the earth as a speck of light is almost commonplace (we've all seen plenty of science fiction films), but for those living during an age in which a journey to the next village was a major undertaking, such an idea represented a truly remarkable insight.

as a way to process complex scientific ideas; in particular, he took the Copernican model, stripped away the mathematics, and explained the fundamentals in terms of readily understood images, which he then used again to take Copernicus into previously unimagined realms.

In this way, Bruno was able to rationalize his theories, even though he used no mathematics. In one of his most farsighted treatises, the Frankfurt Trilogy (*De immenso, De monade,* and *De minimo*), published in 1591, Bruno predated Karl Popper by three and a half centuries when he wrote, "He who desires to philosophize must first of all doubt all things." But rather than spinning his ideas from the yarn of algebra, he molded pictures and manipulated visual images to interpret complex ideas.

Thanks to this shift in the way science is viewed, today many scientists and philosophers believe that mathematics is not the only modeling tool available to them. At the cutting edge is the idea that the way forward, the route to solving the deepest puzzles, may come only from an alignment of intuition, pictorial logic, and equations on a page; in other words, a powerful meshing of Galileo and Bruno.

Giordano Bruno would have approved of this; it was what he struggled for with the limited resources at his disposal. He cared little for practicality and wanted always to get to the root cause of things and then to extrapolate onward and ever farther, toward the stars. Galileo's pool-table world could solve everyday engineering problems, but once removed from the prosaic, his model of the universe was entirely inadequate, entirely unable to explain the true miracle of existence. In some mysterious way, Bruno's form of natural philosophy tapped into the eternal. The Nolan had touched the divine, a fact realized by only a very few while the man was alive.

But other aspects of the Nolan's rational work have made an equal impact. A century after Bruno's death, the great Dutch physicist Christian Huygens found some of Bruno's ideas inspirational but quite properly wished to defer open support until clear evidence could confirm these radical notions. "Later authors such as Cusanus, Brunus [sic], and Kepler have furnished the planets with inhabitants," Huygens wrote in a letter to his brother Constantine. "It is reckoned they require an immense treasury not of twenty or thirty worlds only, but as many as there are grains of sand upon the shore. And yet we say that even this number exceeds that of the Fixed Stars? Some of the Ancients and Jordanus Brunus carry it further, in declaring the number infinite. Indeed, it seems to me certain that the Universe is infinitely extended; but what God has been pleased to place beyond the Region of the Stars, is as much above our knowledge as it is our habitation."[10]

Kepler, too, was a contemporary of Bruno's who was interested in his ideas and even dubbed him "Defender of Infinity." Kepler makes many references to Bruno's ideas, about which he was clearly familiar; more than once he writes favorably of Bruno in the same sentence in which he praises the great fifteenth-century German natural philosopher Nicholas of Cusa and even Galileo Galilei himself.

---

10. Christian Huygens, *The Celestial Worlds Discovered* (London, 1698).

But beyond Bruno's influence as a protean cosmologist, his ideas concerning the art of memory played a significant role in the way this arcane pursuit was adopted and adapted successfully by those born into the age of printing and global travel, people who would otherwise have displayed little interest in the art. The most significant Bruno adept and someone who was undoubtedly fascinated with the entire, dramatic story of Bruno's life was Gottfried Leibniz.

Leibniz, a man who was often referred to as the "Continental Newton," was born in Leipzig forty-six years after Bruno's death. The son of a professor of moral philosophy at the University in Leipzig, Gottfried proved to be a prodigy who gained his doctorate in law by the age of twenty and wrote a paper, *De arte combinatoria* (*On the Art of Combination*), which is now seen as an early theoretical model for the modern computer. Since Leibniz lived in an age when specialization was beginning to overtake the Renaissance model of broad intellectualism, his versatility was rather anachronistic, but because of his great intelligence and dedication he could, even in the late seventeenth century, successfully adopt the mantle of the Renaissance magus.

By the 1670s, Leibniz had become a well-known and respected figure within the European scientific establishment, but he was elevated to celebrity status through his conflict with the most famous and honored scientist in the world, Isaac Newton, then the president of the Royal Society in London. The clash was a priority dispute over a mathematical technique called the calculus. Argument over who had arrived at the technique first, Newton or Leibniz, raged between them for some four decades and even continued between supporters of both after the two scientists were long dead. Today, both men are honored and it is generally agreed that Newton got to the calculus first, but Leibniz devised his technique quite independently and without any knowledge of Newton's work. However, the argument over who should be seen as the father of the calculus is less important than the fact that Leibniz's method was long ago adopted by most scientists.

The calculus is no backwater of science or insignificant tool of the pure mathematician; it is, rather, the single most important mathematical technique known to man. It lies at the heart of most work in science, from biological analysis to civil engineering, from the design of microchips to the plotting of a path to the moon. And Leibniz's method is used instead of Newton's for one very good reason: Newton's system of representing mathematical terms was clumsy and unwieldy, whereas Leibniz's notation was designed for ease of communication and efficiency of use. And this is because Leibniz was steeped in the tradition of memory enhancement using symbols as taught by Bruno.

Yet, important as this undoubtedly was, what Leibniz achieved with his adoption of Bruno's methods was minuscule compared with what he wished to achieve. Leibniz believed in the bold notion that a form of unified knowledge could be found by the application of pure mathematics.

As we have seen, Plato had hinted at this some two millennia before Leibniz, but during the late seventeenth century some mathematicians believed they could see practical ways to determine a purely mathematical model of the universe that would ultimately lead to a union of all knowledge. During the first years of the eighteenth century, Newton, Leibniz's reviled enemy, had led the way with his two great masterpieces, *Principia Mathematica* and *Opticks,* with which he had successfully modeled important aspects of the universe using mathematics. For Newton, the universe was a matrix of geometric figure, integer, and numeric symmetry, and his monumental achievements seemed to confirm this opinion. Leibniz felt precisely the same way about the all-consuming power of mathematics and tried unsuccessfully to describe the entire universe in a set of simple elegant equations all based upon the hierarchy of symbols and images described by Bruno.

It is perhaps ironic that Leibniz's theoretical efforts failed to find a unity of knowledge but helped to develop the propositions offered by the empiricism of Galileo empowered by Newton's mechanics. Among them, these three men produced the greatest impetus for technology and the creation of an industrialized world far from Bruno's spiritual vision.[11]

And Bruno has left his indelible mark elsewhere in areas of the intellect that lie far from science. Best known as a philosopher who, up to that time, did more than any other to visualize the idea of total intellectual freedom, Bruno has been an inspiration for such men as Schelling, Goethe, and most especially Samuel Taylor Coleridge. Like Bruno, each of these men placed freedom and spiritual liberation at the core of their worldview.

---

11. It is interesting to recall that contemporaneously Newton was also led to his great discoveries by a blend of his incomparable talents as an experimenter and his profound understanding of mathematics as well as his knowledge of alchemy and ancient religion. This is discussed at length in my book *Isaac Newton: The Last Sorcerer.*

To these, free religious expression was essential, and they, like Bruno, coupled this sacred belief with unfettered imagination and a will and an energy to push forward the boundaries. In some ways we may think of those who constituted the Romantic Movement of the late eighteenth and early nineteenth centuries as Bruno's kindred spirits. In a sense, men like Coleridge and Goethe were expressing a vision of the world quite different from that offered by the creators of the Industrial Revolution. Steel and steam represented the dark aspect of the age to come, and the Romantics sensed a loss of soul, saw spirit subsumed by smoke, life ground away by cogwheels and the speeding spindle. Goethe and his peers were not so interested in Bruno's picture imagery or even his cosmology; rather, it was his vision of free expression and his belief in universality and infinity that captivated them. And again, the ideal of unified knowledge supported their dreams. But their motivation was not a search for the knowledge that could lead to the making of better machines, nor even to produce a clearer model of how the universe began, how it grew, or what the fundamental rules might be. The Romantics of the nineteenth century were more interested in people, emotions, and utopian visions. For them, Bruno had offered an all-embracing mosaic of ideas, interlinked and mutually supportive; his vision of unification appeared to be the ultimate expression of poetic ecstasy.

And yet amazingly, this resurgence of something of the Renaissance spirit, this radical interpretation, all began with an advertisement in the magazine *Punch* in 1712. An anonymous admirer had offered for sale a copy of Bruno's *Expulsion of the Triumphant*

Beast, a book that had been almost forgotten throughout the seventeenth century. The ad was immensely intriguing and declared (quite inaccurately of course) that the author of the book was "a professed atheist."[12]

The tome was sold, but the purchaser remains unknown. More important, from this advertisement and the brief flurry of interest surrounding the sale, word of Bruno spread. Within a century, Goethe had, in his most famous work, *Faustus*, made repeated references to Bruno and his works; Jacobi and Hegel held heated debates about the merits of the Nolan (Jacobi for and Hegel against); and in a lengthy monograph, part of *Essays for the Fine Arts* (published in 1812), Coleridge wrote of Aristotle, Kant, Plato, and Bruno in the same sentence, comparing the Nolan's brilliance with that of the great ancients. A few years later, in an autobiographical account, Coleridge declared that he had learned the finer points of logic and what he called "dynamic philosophy" from Giordano Bruno.

However, not everyone of the period was so enamored of Bruno and the other cabalists of his day. Hegel wrote: "These men felt themselves dominated, as they really were, by the impulse to create existence and to derive truth from their very selves. They were men of vehement nature, of wild and restless character, of enthusiastic temperament, who could not attain to the calm of knowledge. Though it cannot be denied that there was in them a wonderful insight into what was true and great, there is no doubt

---

12. *Punch* 5, no. 389 (1712), pp. 301–5.

on the other hand that they reveled in all manner of corruption in thought and heart as well as in their outer life."[13]

But probably Bruno's most important contribution to the evolution of nonscientific culture comes again from his work with the art of memory. At the time of Bruno's visit to London between 1583 and 1585, William Shakespeare, just turned twenty, already a father and his wife, Anne Hathaway, pregnant with twins, had recently become an actor in Stratford. He probably did not visit London until after Bruno had departed and the two men almost certainly never met, but there is evidence of links between them.

The connection between Giordano Bruno and William Shakespeare comes via Philip Sidney's friend the poet and occultist Fulke Greville, who knew Bruno well and who appears as a lead character in *The Ash Wednesday Supper*.[14] In a book by David Lloyd entitled *Statesmen and Favourites of England Since the Reformation*, the author offers a eulogy to Greville which includes the passage "One great argument for his worth, was his respect for the worth of others, desiring only to be known to posterity under no other notions than of Shakespeare's and Ben Johnson's Master, Chancellor Egerton's Patron, Bishop Overall's Lord, and Sir Philip Sidney's friend."[15]

---

13. G. W. F. Hegel, *Lectures on the History of Philosophy*, vol. 3 (Oxford, 1936), p. 156.
14. Both Sidney and Greville were independently initiated into occult teaching by no less a figure than John Dee himself.
15. David Lloyd, *Statesmen and Favourites of England Since the Reformation* (1665), quoted in E. K. Chambers, *William Shakespeare*, vol. 2 (Oxford, 1930), p. 250.

This implies that Greville was at some stage Shakespeare's teacher, an idea that is by no means impossible, as Greville's family home was near Stratford-on-Avon and the academically minded Fulke Greville was Shakespeare's senior by ten years. And if we take the argument another stage further, it is perfectly feasible that Greville, a keen follower of Bruno's work, would have passed on to his pupil his appreciation of the Nolan. Furthermore, when Shakespeare arrived in London to start his acting career, it would have been natural for Greville, a leading light on the London literary scene, to introduce the young man to his circle of friends, including occultists and Hermeticists, many of whom were Bruno devotees.

It seems Bruno made a twofold impression on Shakespeare. First, his work and personality made an impact upon the Bard's writing; we can see Bruno on the page and pacing the boards in the guise of several Shakespearean characters. There is Prospero, the isolated magus who dreams of resolving the inner mysteries of the universe, and more directly, the wording of Berowne's famous monologue in praise of love from *Love's Labour's Lost* that mirrors a similar speech from Bruno's *The Expulsion of the Triumphant Beast*.

Bruno also influenced Shakespeare with his skillful use of simple language to evoke complexity of plot and character. The Nolan used the phrase "capturing the voices of the gods" to describe the way in which characters could come alive in a narrative. He caught this spirit well in his own play *Il Candelaio* (*The Torch-Bearer*), published and performed in Paris during 1582 (the year before he left for England), and it demonstrates links with some of Shakespeare's earliest efforts and also with Molière's *Le*

Malade imaginaire and *Le Bourgeois Gentilhomme*. But more important than these connections, Bruno's techniques for developing the power of memory had an enormous effect upon Shakespeare's career, both as an actor and as a playwright.

An actor's life during the sixteenth century was tough. The thespian was poorly paid and received more abuse than respect, it was a peripatetic and often perilous existence, and above all it was intellectually demanding. A play was rarely performed more than two nights in succession, and some parts were long, convoluted, and difficult to learn. Any actor worth his salt was expected to perform several complex roles in one play and to have an extensive repertoire, so that the ability to remember scripts was of paramount importance. Shakespeare was a professional actor for twenty years before he found success as a playwright, and he gained a reputation for his prodigious memory, which was almost certainly developed from a reading of Bruno's works on the art of memory.[16]

However, Bruno's deepest interest and his most powerful ideas came not from his fascination for memory or even pure philosophy but from his religious outlook. His greatest achievement was to blend, to amalgamate seemingly disconnected notions, to fuse science with Christian dogma, Hermeticism with Copernicanism,

---

16. In her book *The Art of Memory* (London, 1992), Dame Frances Yates describes in detail her theory that Shakespeare's Globe Theatre in London was designed according to Hermetic occult rules. The theory suggests that in much the same way the design of their temples was intrinsic to the religious practices of the ancient Egyptians and Greeks, every aspect of the Globe Theatre, from its floor plan to the materials used in its construction, was calculated to energize the performers working there and enhance their memories.

in order to achieve a spiritual gestalt. And for those who read Bruno, his writing was most powerful when he dealt with purely spiritual matters.

Of course, the nature of Bruno's demise and the very fact that the Inquisition hounded him for most of his life created a legend that succeeded in imbuing Bruno's philosophy with heightened drama and dynamism, but this does nothing to diminish the power of his ideas.

Bruno's writing certainly figured large for Spinoza, one of history's most radical religious thinkers. Indeed, one scholar has suggested that the ideas of the two men were at times so close that when Spinoza was writing his classic work *God, Man and His Blessedness,* he must have had opened before him a copy of Bruno's *On Cause, Principle and the One.* Certainly comparisons between the ideas of the two men run deep. Spinoza was said to have been "God-intoxicated," by which it was meant that his sole intellectual drive came from an innate desire to understand the true nature of the divine. Much the same could be said of Bruno. For him, money, family, security, comfort, meant little; his goals were ethereal, intangible.

For the radical religious philosopher, the central principle that emerges from Bruno's teachings is that there is no personal God. Bruno made this most clear when he wrote that "[God] has nothing to do with us except insofar as he imparts himself to the effects of Nature."[17]

---

17. Giordano Bruno, *Opere italiane,* edited by Giovanni Gentile and Vincenzo Spampanato, vol. 2 (Bari, 1925–27), p. 192.

Elsewhere he declared that the myth of the personal extra-mundane God was created by theologians merely for consumption by the uneducated masses and that the educated philosopher and thinker should reject this and adopt the pantheistic position. In *God, Man and His Blessedness,* Spinoza echoed this with the remark "God is indwelling and not the transient cause of things." In other words, according to Spinoza, God created the universe but played no part in its day-to-day running, a notion mirroring Bruno's own analysis.

❦

As he slipped away and the flames consumed him, Bruno set in motion wheels within wheels and sent spinning the cogs of change, for the golden phoenix hovered over Bruno. Throughout his life he had reinvented himself many times, risen from one failure after another to fight another day. In many parts of Europe he had set alight intellectual fires and had moved on when the flames became too hot. So too, in death, his words and ideas resisted the annihilation the cardinals had sought. Indeed, today Bruno's persecutors are largely forgotten, their ideas marginalized. Meanwhile, Bruno's stature has grown; his legacy is now more widely appreciated and honored than at any time during the four centuries since his death. Those four hundred years have led us from a sorry pile of ash in the Field of Flowers to a more tolerant world in which thinkers like Bruno may express their radical views, where challenge is welcomed and embraced, a world in which we may begin to imagine a unity and harmony for which Bruno made the ultimate sacrifice.

Perhaps the most fitting way to end this tale is with Bruno's own words, a passage that amounts to his own epitaph. It is a most poignant passage from one of his last works, *De monade*, published in 1591, the year he returned to Italy. It both expresses his mood as he packed to make his last international journey as a free man and sums up how he viewed his life, his legacy, and his place in the larger scheme of things.

> Much have I struggled. I thought I would be able to
>> conquer . . . And both fate and nature repressed my zeal
>> and my strength.
> Even to have come forth is something, since I see that being
>> able to conquer
> Is placed in the hands of fate.
> However, there was in me whatever I was able to do,
> Which no future century will deny to be mine, that which a
>> victor could have for his own:
> Not to have feared to die, not to have yielded to my equal
> In firmness of nature, and to have preferred a courageous
>> death to a
> Noncombatant life.

BRUNO'S PLACE IN HISTORY

c. 560–c. 480 B.C.:	Pythagoras.
c. 460–c. 370 B.C.:	Democritus.
428–348 B.C.:	Plato.
384–322 B.C.:	Aristotle.
287–212 B.C.:	Archimedes.
c. 250 B.C.:	First records of the library at Alexandria.
A.D. 23–79:	Pliny.
100–170:	Ptolemy.
129–c. 200:	Galen.
second century:	Possible origins of Hermetic texts.
325:	The First Council of Nicaea
c. 450:	Fall of Rome.
c. 450:	Venice founded.
c. 500:	Arabic science becomes organized.
c. 1000:	Florence founded.
1206–80:	Albertus Magnus.
c. 1210–92:	Roger Bacon.
1225–74:	Thomas Aquinas.
1389–1464:	Cosimo de' Medici.

c. 1440:	First printing press.
1449–92:	Lorenzo de' Medici.
1452–1519:	Leonardo da Vinci.
1473–1543:	Copernicus.
1491–1547:	Henry VIII.
1492:	Columbus discovers New World.
1533–1603:	Elizabeth I.
1536–1605:	Clement VIII.
1542–1621:	Robert Bellarmine.
1543:	Copernicus's *De revolutionibus orbium coelestium* published.
1548:	Giordano Bruno born.
1551–89:	Henry III of France.
1561–1626:	Francis Bacon.
1564–1616:	William Shakespeare.
1564–1642:	Galileo.
1571–1630:	Johannes Kepler.
1572:	St. Bartholomew's Day Massacre.
c. 1590:	First scientific society, the Pinelli Circle, founded in Padua.
1596–1650:	René Descartes.
1600:	Bruno burned at the stake.
1609:	Galileo first uses telescope to observe the moon and the satellites of Jupiter.
1616:	*Revolutions* placed on the *Index Librorum Prohibitorum.*
1629–95:	Christian Huygens.
1633:	The trial of Galileo.
1642–1727:	Isaac Newton.
1662:	Royal Society officially formed, London.
1666:	Calculus devised.
1687:	Newton's *Philosophiae Naturalis Principia Mathematica* published.
1704:	Newton's *Opticks* published.

A BRIEF CHRONOLOGY
OF BRUNO'S LIFE

1548:	Born in Nola, near Naples, southern Italy.
1554–63:	Educated in Nola.
1563:	Enters the Monastery of St. Domenico, Naples.
1576:	Leaves monastery when suspected of heresy. Excommunicated *in absentia*.
1576–77:	In Venice and Padua.
1577–79:	Lives for short periods in Rome, Genoa, Noli, Bergamo, Savona, and Turin.
1579:	In Geneva and Lyon. Placed on trial in Geneva by Calvinists, but escapes with a caution.
1579–81:	Teaches in Toulouse, France.
1581–83:	Teaches in France. Spends time in Paris, at the court of King Henry III.

1583–85:	In England, where he may have worked as a spy for Francis Walsingham and lectured at Oxford, and where he wrote many of his most famous books.
1584:	Publishes *The Ash Wednesday Supper* and *The Expulsion of the Triumphant Beast* in England.
1585:	Returns briefly to France.
1586–88:	Teaches in Wittenberg, Germany.
1588–90:	Lives and works in Prague and Helmstedt.
1590–91:	Lives in Frankfurt and Zurich.
Autumn 1591:	Travels to Venice at the invitation of Giovanni Mocenigo.
November 1591–March 1592:	Teaches at the University of Padua.
May 1592:	Arrested by the Venetian Inquisition and placed on trial.
February 1593:	Incarcerated in the prison of the Roman Inquisition.
February 19, 1600:	Burned at the stake in the Field of Flowers, Rome.

BRUNO'S IMPORTANT WORKS

Date of publication	City of publication	Title and brief description
1572	Naples?	*De arca Noe* (*Noah's Ark*).
No later than 1576–81 (now lost)		*De sfera.* A course of lectures given in Toulouse.
1576 (now lost)	Venice	*De' segni de' tempi.* A philosophical tract mentioned by Bruno during the Venetian trial.
1581	Paris	*Clavis magna* (*The Great Key*). Bruno's first mature study of memory.
1582	Paris	*Ars memoriae.* Bruno's first work on the art of memory.

Date of publication	City of publication	Title and brief description
1582	Paris	*Cantus circaeus.* Another work on the art of memory.
1582	Paris	*De compendiosa architectura et complemento artis Lullii.* A further work on memory linked with the ideas of Raymond Lull.
1582	Paris	*De umbris idearum (The Shadow of Ideas).* Mnemonics.
1582	Paris	*Cantus Circaeus ad eam memoriae praxim ordinatus quam ipse ludiciarum appellat (The Chant of Circe).* Mnemonics.
1582	Paris	*Il Candelaio (The Torch-Bearer).* A satirical play.
1583	Paris	*Ars reminiscendi et in phantastico campo exarandi (The Art of Recollection).* Mnemonics.
1584	London	*La cena de le ceneri (The Ash Wednesday Supper).* A narrative in which Bruno's ideas on cosmology and infinity are expounded.

Date of publication	City of publication	Title and brief description
1584	London	*De la causa, principio et uno* (*On Cause, Principle and the One*). Another treatise on infinity and cosmology.
1584	London	*De l'infinito universo et mondi* (*On the Infinite Universe and Its worlds*). Cosmology and universal Copernicanism.
1584	London	*Spaccio de la bestia trionfante* (*The Expulsion of the Triumphant Beast*). A philosophical treatise explaining Bruno's radical spiritual model.
1585	Paris	*De gli eroici fuiri* (unpublished).
1587	Paris	*Lampas triginta statarum* (*The Lamp of Thirty Statues*). Mnemonics.
1587	Paris	*De lampade combinatoria Lulliana* (*The Combination Lamp of Raymond Lull*). A book on the art of memory.
1590	Helmstedt	*De magia* (*On Magic*).

Date of publication	City of publication	Title and brief description
1591	Frankfurt	*De imaginum, signorum et idearum compositione, ad omnia, inventionum, dispositonum et memoriae genera* (*On the Composition of Images, Signs and Ideas*). Mnemonics.
1591	Frankfurt	The Frankfurt Trilogy: *De immenso, De monade,* and *De minimo.* A summation of Brunian philosophy.
1591	A draft published in Frankfurt in 1590, and another in Padua (1591).	*De vinculis in genere* (*Of Links in General*). Incomplete. A summation of Bruno's philosophy and religious opinions.
Unknown No later than 1584	Unknown (probably London)	*Sigillus sigillorum* (Seal of Seals).

BIBLIOGRAPHY

Baigent, Michael, and Richard Leigh. *The Inquisition.* New York, 1999.

Berti, Domenico. *Vita di Giordano Bruno de Nola.* Turin, 1868.

Bossy, John. *Giordano Bruno and the Embassy Affair.* New Haven, Conn., 1991.

Bruno, Giordano. *The Ash Wednesday Supper.* Edited and translated by Edward A. Gosselin and Lawrence S. Lerner. Toronto, 1977.

Bruno, Giordano. *The Expulsion of the Triumphant Beast.* Edited and translated by Arthur D. Imerti. Lincoln, Neb., 1992.

Bruno, Giordano. *Opere italiane.* 3 vols. Edited by Giovanni Gentile and Vincenzo Spampanato. Bari, 1925–27.

Boulting, William. *Giordano Bruno: His Life, Thought and Martyrdom.* London, 1914.

Chamberlin, E. R. *The World of the Italian Renaissance.* London, 1982.

Cochrane, Eric. *Italy 1530–1630.* London, 1988.

Cohn-Sherbok, Lavinia. *Who's Who in Christianity.* London, 1998.

Favaro, E., ed. *Galileo Galilei.* Florence, 1890–1909.

Firpo, Luigi. *Gli scritti di Francesco Pucci.* Turin, 1957.

Firpo, Luigi. "Il processo di Giordano Bruno." Rome, 1993 (unpublished).

Franzoi, Umberto. *The Prisons of the Doges' Palace in Venice.* Milan, 1997.

Fowler, Alastair. *Time's Purpled Masquers: Stars and the Afterlife in Renaissance English Literature.* New York, 1996.

Fumerton, Patricia, and Simon Hunt, eds. *Renaissance Culture and the Everyday.* Philadelphia, 1999.

Gatti, Hilary. *Giordano Bruno and Renaissance Science.* Ithaca, N.Y., 1998.

Gentile, Giovanni. *Documenti della vita di Giordano Bruno.* Florence, 1933.

Greenberg, Sidney, trans. *The Infinite in Giordano Bruno.* New York, 1950.

Gui, Bernard. *Manuel de l'inquisiteur.* Trans. G. Mollat. Paris, 1969.

Hall, A. Rupert. *From Galileo to Newton.* New York, 1981.

Hegel, G. W. F. *Lectures on the History of Philosophy.* Vol. 3. Oxford, 1936.

Holden, Anthony. *William Shakespeare: His Life and Work.* Boston, 1999.

Huygens, Christian. *The Celestial Worlds Discovered.* London, 1698.

Kristeller, P. O. *Eight Philosophers of the Italian Renaissance.* Stanford, Calif., 1964.

Lloyd, David. *Statesmen and Favourites of England Since the Reformation,* 1665. Quoted in E. K. Chambers, *William Shakespeare,* vol. 2. Oxford, 1930.

Mackay, Charles. "The Alchemysts." In *Memoirs of Extraordinary Popular Delusions,* by Richard Bentley. London, 1841.

Manchester, William. *A World Lit Only by Fire: The Medieval Mind and the Renaissance.* Boston, 1992.

Merback, Mitchell B. *The Thief, the Cross and the Wheel: Pain and the Spectacle of Punishment in Medieval and Renaissance Europe.* London, 1999.

Mercati, Angelo. *Il sommario del processo di Giordano Bruno.* Vatican City, 1942.

Naphy, William G., ed. and trans. *Documents on the Continental Reformation.* New York, 1996.

Naudé, Gabriel. *Instruction à la France sur la vérité de l'histoire des Frères de la Rose-Croix.* Paris, 1623.

Norwich, John Julius. *A History of Venice.* London, 1983.

Partner, Peter. *The Murdered Magicians.* London, 1987.

Procacci, Giuliano. *History of the Italian People.* London, 1991.

Rosenthal, Margaret F. *The Honest Courtesan.* Chicago, 1992.

Rossetti, Lucia. *The University of Padua.* Padua, 1999.

Singer, Dorothy. *Giordano Bruno: His Life and Thought.* New York, 1950.

Spampanato, Vincenzo. *Vita di Giordano Bruno.* Messina, 1921.

Stewart, Ian A. *Philip Sidney: A Double Life.* London, 1999.

Thorndike, Lynn. *A History of Magic and Experimental Science.* Vol. 7. New York, 1958.

Trevor-Roper, H. R. *The European Witch-Craze of the Sixteenth and Seventeenth Centuries.* London, 1967.

White, Michael. *Isaac Newton: The Last Sorcerer.* London, 1997.

White, Michael. *Leonardo: The First Scientist.* Boston, 2000.

Yates, Frances A. *The Art of Memory.* London, 1992.

Yates, Frances A. *Giordano Bruno and the Hermetic Tradition.* Chicago, 1964.

Yates, Frances A. *The Rosicrucian Enlightenment.* London, 1972.

USEFUL WEBSITES

The Net provides literally thousands of Bruno websites. Here is a very small sample of some of the more informative ones.

The Folly of Giordano Bruno
www-astronomy.mps.html

Giordano Bruno: Father of the Modern Universe
www.users.nais.com/-thack/bruno.html

New Advent
www.newadvent.org/cathen/03016a.html

Giordano Bruno
www.Es.rice.edu/ES/humsoc/Galileo/Catalog/Files/bruno.html

Biography of Giordano Bruno
www.setileague.org/awards/brunoquo.html

Erin Looney on Giordano Bruno
www.honors.unr.edu/fenimore/wt202/looney.html

Giordano Bruno (1998) by John Patrick Michael Murphy
www.infidels.org/library/modern/john_murphy/giordanobruno.html

Science and Human Values: Bruno, Brahe and Kepler, Prof. Fred L. Wilson
www.rit/edu/-flwstv/bruno.html

Giordano Bruno: The Forgotten Philosopher
www.aracnet.com/-atheist/hist/bruno.html

Giordano Bruno: World Socialist Website
www.wsws.org/articles/2000/feb2000/brun-fI6.shtml

Giordano Bruno: Pantheist Martyr
www.members.aol.com/pantheism)/brunlife.html

The Harbinger
www.entropy.me.usouthal.edu/harbinger/xvi/9/iii/btrx.html

The History Guide: Lectures on Modern European Intellectual History
www.pagesz.net/stevek/intellect/lecture 8a.html

INDEX

4/09 12   11/07